Joe DiMaggio

Joe DiMaggio

A BIOGRAPHY

BY GENE SCHOOR

DOUBLEDAY & COMPANY, INC.
GARDEN CITY, NEW YORK

Library of Congress Cataloging in Publication Data

Schoor, Gene.
  Joe DiMaggio: a biography.

  Includes index.
  SUMMARY: A biography of the famous ballplayer from his childhood
to his retirement from baseball.
    1. DiMaggio, Joseph Paul, 1914–   —Juvenile literature. 2. Base-
ball players—United States—Biography—Juvenile literature. [1. DiMag-
gio, Joseph Paul, 1914–   2. Baseball players] I. Title.
GV865.D5S27   796.357′092′4 [B] [92]
ISBN: 0-385-12290-x Trade
      0-385-12291-8 Prebound
Library of Congress Catalog Card Number 79-7700

This book is dedicated to three of DiMaggio's most rabid fans . . .

> Gabey and Danny Feder
> and
> Yoni Schwartz. . . .

Joe DiMaggio

1

May 15, 1941, was a fine day at Yankee Stadium. The fans, many of them in shirt sleeves, were patiently waiting for the game to start between the Yankees and the Chicago White Sox. Though World War II was raging all over Europe, and the United States had begun drafting all eligible men into the Army, the Stadium crowd was in a rather happy mood.

It was a feeling, however, not shared at the moment in the locker room of the New York Yankees. They were bogged down in fourth place, 5½ games behind the league-leading Cleveland Indians. And they showed little evidence of being able to better that position.

The big reason for the Yankees' doldrums was Joe DiMaggio's batting slump. Now, just a few minutes before game time, Joe was trying to relax by reading his favorite comic book, *Superman*, in front of his locker. His long, lean legs stretched out before him, Joe calmly sat there puffing slowly on a cigarette.

Sports Editor Max Kase of the New York *Journal-American,* visiting in the dressing room, pointed to the book. "Anything's better than reading your batting average this year, eh, Joe?"

"You said it, Max," Joe agreed. "I don't even look at that anymore. What am I hitting now, anyway? Anybody know?"

Kase checked his notebook. "It's .299."

DiMaggio grunted. "I didn't think it was that high. I can't buy a hit lately. I just can't seem to get going."

"I'll tell you something else, Joe," the *Journal-American* sports editor continued. "You know for the past twenty games you've been hitting only .184? If you hadn't started the season with a tremendous splurge that's about what you'd be hitting altogether now."

Joe shook his head. "I've been pressing too much."

"What happened to you all of a sudden, Joe?" Kase asked. "You hit in every game of the exhibition season; you started off hitting in the first eight games when the regular season opened; then all of a sudden—nothing!"

"It was McCrabb of the Athletics who did it," Joe growled. "All day he kept pitching me dinky little curves and the changeups. He threw me off stride, made me lose my timing. I didn't get a hit that day and I haven't had many since then, either. I can't seem to get that rhythm back in my swing."

"Well, maybe today's the day, Joe. A hitter like you has got to break out sometime."

"Who's going for the Sox, you know?" Joe asked.

"Ed Smith."

Joe nodded. "A left-hander." He shrugged. "Who knows? Maybe I'll get one today."

Manager Joe McCarthy walked into the room. "Let's go, guys. On the field."

DiMaggio stood up, moved his shoulders to loosen the muscles. "Well, here goes nothin'."

As it turned out, it wasn't anything to get excited about. Joe managed to reach the White Sox hurler for one single in his four times at bat. But at least he hadn't drawn the "horse collar" again, as he had in nearly half of the past twenty games.

The next day, against the White Sox, DiMaggio broke loose with a triple and a home run. In the final game of the series with the Chicago club he singled and walked in four trips to the plate. He was beginning to feel better about things.

The St. Louis Browns came to the Stadium next, and DiMaggio celebrated their arrival with a three-for-three day, two singles and a double. The next day he got one hit, a double, the next game a single. The Detroit Tigers came to town and Joe hit in three straight games against them. And suddenly he caught fire, and as he began to hit, the rest of the club emerged from its doldrums and the team burst alive. It happened almost overnight.

It looked for a while as if Joe could not be stopped. He got one single in each of three games against the Red Sox. Then he personally took care of the Washington Senators, getting six hits in the three-game series, including a home run and a triple, and winning two of the games with his timely hits.

Except for the fact that he was hitting again, and the Yankees once more were contenders for the league lead, no one paid particular attention to Joe's phenomenal hitting.

But by the time Joe's hitting streak reached twenty games, the press began to take notice. When it hit thirty it began getting nationwide attention, and the pressure and tension began to mount. Just as it was in San Francisco in 1934, when he was setting the sixty-one-game Pacific Coast League record, Joe became the special target for enemy pitchers. Each wanted to be the man to stop the streak.

They began to pitch him more carefully, trying to keep the ball on the corners, wanting to give him nothing too good to hit at. A little extra snap went on to the curves, a little more jump on the fast ones. But DiMaggio would not be denied.

On June 20 he walloped Tiger hurlers Bobo Newsom and Archie McKain for four straight hits, and the first record was passed. In the clubhouse after the game, won by the Yankees on Joe's great hitting, several of the players surrounded him as he undressed in front of his locker.

"Congratulations, Joe," third baseman Red Rolfe said.

DiMaggio turned around, puzzled. "What for, Red?"

Rolfe grinned. "You know you passed Rogers Hornsby's streak of hitting in thirty-three straight games today. This was a real big one, Joe."

Joe looked surprised. "No! I hadn't been counting, anyway. I'm afraid to. Just let me keep hitting. Let somebody else do the counting."

Keep hitting is just what Joe did, and everyone was counting the games. Silently now, though, lest they jinx the player by talking out loud about breaking records.

By June 28, DiMaggio had hit in thirty-nine straight games. George Sisler's modern record of forty-one was just around the corner. This day Johnny Babich, who had always been a tough opponent, was to pitch for the Philadelphia Athletics.

Joe, batting fourth in the lineup, got a chance to hit in the first inning when Tommy Henrich singled. Joe felt the suspense in the air as he strode to the plate. The ball park grew silent. He tried to shake off the tension by stalling and waving a couple of bats back and forth. But he couldn't put out of his mind the fact that he was on the verge of a record-breaking hitting streak. Tension began to knot his stomach.

He set himself at the plate and waited for Babich to pitch. The Athletics' hurler looked back at Henrich leading off first, stretched, then came down to DiMaggio with a curve outside, ball one. The next pitch was another curve, high outside. Ball two. Babich came back again outside for ball three. Three balls and no strikes.

DiMaggio looked down at the third-base coach for the sign. He blinked, looked again. The "hit" sign was on! Joe smiled to himself. Good old Joe McCarthy. The Yankee manager, wanting to give Joe every possible chance to extend the hitting streak, was giving Joe permission to hit the three-and-nothing pitch a hurler usually aims right down the middle, knowing the batter will almost always let the ball go by.

But Babich wasn't giving anything away today. The fourth pitch was way outside and Joe walked. Well, he thought, as he trotted down to first, it's only the first inning.

Now it was the fourth inning, and Joe was at bat for the second time. Anxious as he was to get a hit, DiMaggio still refused to offer at the bad pitches Babich threw. On four straight balls he walked for the second straight time.

It was the seventh inning now and the tension was terrific as Joe stepped in for his third time at bat. Babich went into his windup and threw a curve that came down high and outside, almost out of Joe's reach. Joe lunged after the pitch and cracked a sizzling drive right back at the pitcher. The ball shot past Babich's legs like a rifle bullet and into center field for a clean single. That made it forty straight games as the crowd roared its approval.

The next day the Yankees journeyed to Washington for a double-header with the Senators. Dutch Leonard started the first game for the Washington team. Dutch was having one of his better years with the Senators, and was tough when he was right.

For four innings Leonard matched scoreless innings with Yankee hurler Red Ruffing. But the Yankees broke through Leonard in the fifth, scoring three runs, and in the sixth DiMaggio, hitless, came to bat for the third time. Leonard's first pitch was a fast ball right across the plate and Joe flashed his big bat and drove the ball sharply into left-center field. Speedy left-fielder George Washington Case took after the ball. Cramer came over from center field for it. But the ball dropped safely between them! DiMaggio sped around first base and tore into second before the ball was retrieved.

Joe had tied George Sisler's modern major-league record of hitting in forty-one straight games. Sisler's record had stood since 1922. News and motion-picture cameras, on hand for the eventuality, ground away as DiMaggio tipped his hat to the crowd's cheers. Moments later, he raced around the bases and scored on a passed ball that got by the Senators' catcher. Joe Gordon, the next Yankee batter, gripped his hand as he crossed the plate, and the Yankees, to a man, ran out of the dugout and led him back to the bench, pummeling him on the back and shouting their congratulations.

The Yankees went on to win that game, 9–4. But there was a second game to play that day, and a chance for Joe to set a new record.

Charlie Stanceau was going on the mound for the Yankees for this game, against Sid Hudson for the Senators. But DiMaggio had a new worry to add to his tension. A fan, wandering onto the field between games, had stolen his favorite bat! Joe had been using the same bat since he started the hitting streak on May 15. He had even marked the handle with green indelible pencil so that the other players would know it was his "lucky" bat and not use it. Now it was gone, taken by an inconsiderate souvenir hunter.

In the dugout, Joe poured out his rage, the other players keeping silent. It was a bad omen, they knew. And indeed it began to look that way when the game started. The Yankees scored twice in the first inning off Hudson, but DiMaggio popped out during the rally.

In the third inning, he bounced weakly to third base. In the fifth he popped up again. The players fidgeted on the bench and the crowd began to murmur. Joe tried to look unconcerned, but the tremendous strain was showing on his usually "dead pan" face. He was scowling and muttering to himself, and he paced back and forth in the Yankee dugout.

In the seventh inning, up for the fourth time, Joe rifled the ball into left field for a clean single! The crowd leaped to its feet and cheered wildly. The Yankee bench roared its happiness, the players jumping up and shaking their fists in the air.

Now there was one record left to fall—the one Wee Willie Keeler set in 1897, when he hit in forty-four straight games. That was made before modern major-league baseball, though, when a foul ball was not counted as a strike and the hitter had a better chance at the plate.

It was the Yankee Stadium again, this time a hot, muggy July 1, and the Boston Red Sox were in town for a double-header. A hit in both games and Joe would tie the all-time record of Keeler's. A great crowd of over sixty thousand jammed the Stadium, braving the terrific heat, to root for DiMaggio to come through.

The Yankees bombarded left-hander Mickey Harris out of the box in the fourth inning with a four-run rally, and DiMaggio led off in the fifth inning against relief hurler Mike Ryba. The Red Sox pitcher, working carefully, sent the count to three balls and two strikes. Then Joe chopped a high bounder toward third. It was a tough play for third baseman, Jim Tabor. He charged in at the slow-hit ball, grabbed it with his bare hand, and threw to first—wildly—and Joe sped on to second base! In the press box, however, everyone craned his head to look at Dan Daniel, sportswriter for the New York *World-Telegram*, who was official scorer at the Stadium that season. Daniel smiled and held up one finger, indicating that it was a clean hit.

Even DiMaggio, standing on second, didn't know whether he had been credited with a hit or Tabor with an error. But, Joe admitted later, he wondered about it while standing on second. And he felt uncomfortable, too, for though the ball was a tough chance for Tabor, and he had had to hurry his throw, Joe felt that it wasn't a clean hit. And he didn't want his streak to stay alive on the gift of an official scorer.

Fortunately, in the next inning Joe smacked a one-one pitch to left for a solid single. All doubts were erased now, and the fans cheered Joe deafeningly when he took his place in center field at the end of the inning.

One more game to go to tie Keeler's record. The Yankees had won the first game of the double-header, 7–2, and the Red Sox sent Jack Wilson in to try to stop them in the second game. Joe wasted no time here. He smacked one of Wilson's fast balls for a single in the first inning—and the Keeler mark was tied!

Forty-four straight games! A hit tomorrow in the final game against the Red Sox and Joe would go down in history—a new king of the hitters.

Joe had a kind of premonition about this one, however. Heber Newsome was scheduled to pitch for the Red Sox, a hurler DiMaggio had never hit too well. He rubbed his chin thoughtfully in the locker room before the game. "I got a feeling about this one, Lefty," he said.

"G'wan," Lefty Gomez scoffed. "Stop thinking so much. It's not a healthy thing for a ballplayer."

As Joe came to bat the first time, a great cheer went up from the stands. But then the fans suddenly grew silent as Newsome began his windup and DiMaggio set himself in the batter's box. Newsome missed the plate the first time but his next pitch was a fast ball across the letters. Joe swung—and the bat felt good as he hit the ball solidly to right-center field. Stan Spence, the right fielder, raced deep to right center and made a diving catch of the drive.

In the third inning Joe lined sharply to third baseman Jim Tabor. Joe was twice up, twice down after hitting the ball sharply. Joe shook his head. He was right, he thought. Newsome would be the one to stop him.

Joe came up next in the fifth inning, while the Yankees

were in the middle of a rally against Newsome. Red Rolfe
was on first, with one out. Newsome got ahead of Joe, one
ball and two strikes. Then he tried to pour a fast ball
through. Joe swung—and the sharp crack brought the
crowd to its feet. The ball sailed high and far into left
field. It hit well up into the left-field stands for a home
run! That was it, a new record of forty-five straight
games! Rolfe, the runner on base, touched home plate
and waited for DiMaggio to come around. As Joe crossed
home, Rolfe grabbed him in a bear hug, and the rest of
the Yankees crowded around to shake Joe's hand and
pound him on the back.

The Yankees won the game, 8–4. It was Joe's eight-
eenth homer of the year, his thirteenth of the hitting
streak, and his one hundredth hit of the year.

The Yankees were off the next day. DiMaggio rested at
home with his wife, Dorothy, who was pregnant at the
time. Every news program blared out that DiMag would
try to continue his consecutive-game hitting streak.

It had become one of the most important events in
America. A front-page story. Each day after Joe D's hit or
hits, news of it spread like wildfire into the nation's
homes, factories, schools. Bandleader Les Brown of the
Bob Hope radio show even introduced a song, "Joltin' Joe
DiMaggio," celebrating the fantastic Joe. It got a lot of
play on radio throughout the nation that summer.

And now, hundreds of wires, letters, and congrat-
ulatory phone calls began pouring into Yankee Stadium.
Sportswriters and editors dogged his footsteps wherever
Joe went. They badgered him as he went to and from the
ball park. They waited for him in the lobby of his hotel.

Eager Yankee fans followed him around New York City. He was the biggest celebrity in the biggest city in the world.

All of DiMaggio's teammates, too, were part of the nerve-racking scene as they became caught up in the excitement of the greatest hitting streak in baseball, and all of them were becoming nervous wrecks with the tension. But for all the near hysteria surrounding his every move, Joe managed to remain outwardly calm.

The pressure continued on DiMaggio, even though he had racked up a new record. Every day now he added to the record. Forty-six, forty-seven, forty-eight. Would the streak never end? The Philadelphia Athletics came to the Stadium, and DiMaggio ran his streak to forty-nine straight, getting seven hits in the next three games: four singles, a double, a triple, and a home run.

The St. Louis Browns were his next victims, then four games with the White Sox and the streak was fifty-five games.

The Yankees went into Cleveland territory now, and Joe went three-for-four to beat the Indians, making it fifty-six straight games.

Then it was July 17 and a night game was scheduled with the Indians. The air seemed so tense that Joe could hardly breathe. He was edgy, wondering how long he could continue his streak. Sometimes he thought it would be a relief to be back to normal again. He had a light snack in the hotel about dinnertime and, together with Lefty Gomez, grabbed a cab to the Cleveland ball park.

The cab driver, naturally, began talking about the ball game, though he didn't recognize his passengers as players. Then, as he stopped for a red light, he turned around and took a good look at the men. He appeared startled. "Hey, Joe DiMaggio! And Lefty Gomez!"

Gomez grinned. "Who'd you think it was, the Smith brothers?"

The driver shook his head. "I hate to tell you this, Joe, but I was telling my wife tonight, 'Honey,' I said, 'I think they're finally gonna stop DiMag' tonight.' I hope I'm wrong, Joe, but my hunches are usually right."

Gomez roared at the driver like an enraged bull. "What are you trying to do, jinx him?"

"Aw, you don't believe in jinxes, do you, Lefty?" Joe said. But truthfully, he was disturbed himself.

The largest crowd ever to view a night game at that time—over sixty-seven thousand fans—jammed Municipal Stadium for the contest. Al Smith, a left-hander, was slated to pitch for the Indians against Lefty Gomez for the Yankees.

In the first inning against Smith, Joe smashed a hot grounder down the third-base line. Ken Keltner, the great Cleveland third baseman, sped over to the line, made a backhand stop of the smash, and threw across the diamond to nip Joe by a step.

In the fourth frame, Smith walked DiMaggio on a three-two pitch. The tension began to mount again, as it always did in the late innings when Joe still hadn't gotten his hit.

The score was 1–1 when Joe came to bat again in the seventh. The way Smith was pitching, this might be his last time at the plate. The Cleveland left-hander came through with a strike. Then a ball. Another strike, then Joe slammed another scorcher along the third-base line.

Again Keltner went to the line, again he made a sensational backhand stab of the hot grounder, then threw to first to get DiMaggio.

Joe sat down on the bench disgustedly. "That Keltner's murdering me," he said to Tommy Henrich.

In the eighth the Yankees started another rally, routing Smith from the mound. Two runs were in, the score was 4–1, the bases loaded, and Jim Bagby came on in relief to face DiMaggio.

A hush fell over the giant stadium. You could hear a pin drop in the stands. This was undoubtedly DiMaggio's last time at bat. Bagby finished his warmup tosses and signaled to the plate umpire that he was ready. DiMaggio stepped into the batter's box, set himself in his wide stance, the bat cocked over his right shoulder, his features set and emotionless.

Bagby toed the rubber and went to work. He took his full windup. The pitch came down, a fast curve low, ball one. Bagby hitched at his belt and bent down for the sign from his batterymate. He wound up, pitched, and Joe swung and missed. Strike one.

The duel continued. Bagby stepped off the rubber and began rubbing the ball between his hands. DiMaggio waited, anxious, unmoving. Bagby stepped on again and looked down at the hitter. He shook off the sign from the catcher. He shook off another one. Then he began his windup. But Joe was tired of waiting and stepped out of the box, an automatic time out. He wasn't going to let Bagby get him too tense. Both men were ready now. Bagby wound up, twisted, threw. Joe's bat flashed and the crowd roared at the crack. It was a ground ball near shortstop. Lou Boudreau glided over, grabbed the ball,

flipped to Ray Mack at second. Then Mack threw to
Oscar Grimes at first in time for the double play on
DiMaggio!

A great roar went up from the crowd. The fans knew
the streak was over. As Joe trotted slowly to his outfield
post, they stood up all over the Stadium and for fully five
minutes gave him one of the greatest ovations ever heard
in baseball.

When the records were tabulated, it turned out to be
the most amazing streak in baseball history. He had hit in
56 straight games, 57 if you wanted to count the single he
hit in the All-Star game during the streak.

Joe had gone up at bat 223 times, gotten 91 hits for an
average of .408. His hits were good for a total of 160 total
bases; 16 doubles, 4 triples, and 15 home runs were
among the safe blows. He scored 56 runs, drove in 55
more, walked 21 times, struck out only 7 times, and twice
was hit by the pitcher.

It was more than just a personal streak, though. When
it started, the Yankees were in fourth place, 5½ games
behind the league-leading Cleveland Indians. When Joe
was finally stopped, in a game the Yankees won, 4–3, the
New Yorkers were in first place, 7 games ahead of the
same Indians. The Yankees had just about wrapped up
the pennant on the momentum provided by the greatest
hitting streak in baseball.

The day after Smith and Bagby—and yes, Keltner, too—
stopped him, Joe took off on another streak, this time
good for 16 straight games. If he had not been stopped
that night in Cleveland, the streak would have gone 73
games.

Baseball, after all, is big business. And baseball players

generally are an unsentimental lot. But not this time. On the night of August 29, Joe's teammates let him know how they felt about him.

That night the Yankees had just checked in at the Hotel Shoreham for a series with Washington starting the next day. Immediately George Selkirk got on the house phone, setting into motion a plan that had been prepared with the team for days.

Selkirk called all the players and the sportswriters who were traveling with the club. "Come down to my room in half an hour," he said. "Room 609-D. Everything's all set."

The players and the writers all gathered in Selkirk's room on time. Everyone was there now except DiMaggio and his roommate, Lefty Gomez. It was up to Lefty to entice Joe into Selkirk's room without getting him suspicious.

Gomez, wanting to make sure everyone would be there when he arrived with Joe, was stalling as long as possible. Lefty combed his hair, then recombed it. He tied his tie, took it off, and selected another one. Joe was getting impatient.

"Good grief, Lefty!" he exclaimed. "I never saw a guy take so long to get dressed. Come on already, willya?"

"Don't worry, don't worry, I'll soon be finished," Gomez soothed. Finally he felt it was time.

"Say, Joe, I got to pick something up in Selkirk's room on the way down. C'mon along."

Joe balked. "Naah, I'll meet you in the lobby."

"C'mon, willya?" Gomez urged. "It's right down the hall. It'll just take me a second."

"All right, all right," Joe agreed. "But let's make it fast, huh? I want to get downstairs."

The players were waiting. Selkirk was at the door to his room, keeping watch. When he saw the pair coming, he closed the door and turned to the crowd in the room. "Sssh, they're coming." When DiMaggio and Gomez walked in, everyone began jabbering at Joe at once.

"What took you so long? What's the idea of being so late?"

Joe looked around at his teammates and the writers. He seemed confused. Then the Yankees burst out loudly with "For He's a Jolly Good Fellow," followed by a hip-hip-hooray, led by Frankie Crosetti.

Then Gomez presented Joe with a gift. "Go ahead, Joe," he said quietly. "Open it."

DiMaggio looked down at the box, then at his teammates, swallowed, and slowly unwrapped the package. It was a silver humidor. The top bore a likeness of Joe finishing a swing. There were numbers on either side—56 for the number of consecutive games hit in, and 91 for the total number of hits made. On the front was an engraved inscription. "Read it out loud, Joe," Crosetti said.

Joe read it hesitantly. "Presented to Joe DiMaggio by his fellow players on the New York Yankees to express their great admiration for his consecutive-game hitting record, 1941."

DiMaggio bit his lip hard. "Thanks, fellows," he said humbly. "This is swell. Only I didn't think you guys liked me."

Then, to relieve his embarrassment, Joe lifted the humidor, which was filled, and began walking around the room. "Cigars, cigarettes!" he called. "Get your scorecard here!"

But all could see that he was flustered at the ceremony.

Joe Gordon finally relieved the pressure. "Hey," he shouted, "you know this is the first time Gomez ever kept a secret!"

Everybody laughed then, relaxing a little, and Bill Dickey suggested a toast. Johnny Murphy gave it. "Joe," he said solemnly, "we want to let you know how proud we are to be playing on the same ball club with you, and that we think your great hitting streak spurred us on to a pennant."

Recently, looking back at that boisterous ceremony, Joe said, "When Lefty Gomez, turned the handle of that door in the Shoreham, it was the greatest thrill I've ever had in baseball, bigger than when I broke any batting record or hit any World Series home run. It's great to know that the guys you work with think you're a regular guy, too. I'll never forget that night in my life."

2

The fog rolled in silently off the bay, wet and cool, a dirty gray blanket that settled swiftly in thick folds over the city, dimming the street lamps to a feeble glow, hiding the approaching dawn with its density.

The city of San Francisco was quiet, content to sleep under its dark coverlet. For soon enough the fog would lift, and the midsummer sun would rise, hot and red, and the city would awaken, heavy-lidded and weary, to start another day.

But now it was still dark. Then, on Taylor Street, above Fisherman's Wharf, a light showed suddenly in the ground-floor apartment of No. 2047, a three-story frame-and-stucco structure exactly like all the houses that climbed in an unbroken line up Taylor Street to the top of the hill. In the bedroom of the small apartment Giuseppe DiMaggio rose from his bed and began to dress. He listened a moment in the stillness of the room, hearing the faint, lonely clanking of the bell buoys as they rolled gently on the rhythmic tide. Then, from the kitchen, where his wife, Rosalie, was preparing his breakfast, there came the appetizing aroma of strong coffee, freshly brewed and he felt hungry.

"Are the boys up, Rosa?" Giuseppe asked his wife when he entered the kitchen. He walked to the sink without waiting for her answer, splashed cold water on his face, and dried himself on the towel that hung on a wooden bar on the wall at his side.

"Yes, Papa. They are up. They get dressed."

"Giuseppe, too?" He turned from the sink and looked at her. She didn't answer.

"Not Giuseppe, eh?" His voice, thick with the accent of his native Sicily, was filled with scorn.

"His brothers can help their papa on the boat. His sisters can help to clean—and to fix the nets. But not Giuseppe. No, to help his papa to fish for crabs it is too good, eh?"

Mrs. DiMaggio looked at her husband. She saw his face, angry now beneath the smooth black hair, the skin rough and windburned, the eyes lined deeply around the corners from long years of squinting into the glare of sun-reflecting water. He was a good man.

"No, Papa," she said to him. "You know it is not like that with little Giuseppe. He wants to help. He is a good boy. But the boat makes him sick when the sea is bad, and even when it is not so bad. And the smell of the fish, it makes him sick, too." She shrugged, smiling with motherly tolerance. "He is not a fisherman. Maybe when he gets big, he will fish."

"What is he, then?" challenged her husband, and his voice was angry. "I'll tell you what he is, Rosa. He is a no-good. A loafer. To run and play with the other no-goods in the street he is never sick. To play that what-you-call-it, baseball, and tear his pants and his shoes, for this he is never sick." He slammed his cup on the table and shook his head.

"I'm telling you, Rosa. That boy's never gonna be no good! Never."

Rosalie DiMaggio sighed deeply. This was an old argument between them. "Papa," she said gently, "how do you talk that way about your own boy? He's only ten years old. In America it's different from Sicily. A boy likes to play with the other boys. He doesn't like to work, work all the time. You'll see. He'll be a little older, he'll work, too."

Her husband waved his hand to deride her argument as he swallowed a mouthful of his breakfast. "Don't make no excuse for the boy, Rosa. He's plenty old enough to work after school like his brothers. Dominic is how old—seven? —and he's always running home from school to help his papa. And Thomas and Michael and Vincent, when they were younger than Giuseppe they went out on the boat with me. No, he's just a lazy boy, Rosa," Giuseppe Di-Maggio said to his wife, "and he don't listen, he don't talk. He just sits there and looks angry. All the time—he no talk."

"Well, maybe you're right, Papa," she acknowledged. "But he says he's sick when he goes near the fish. Who can say if it's so or not?"

"I can say," her husband retorted. "For two hundred, three hundred years the DiMaggios been fishermen in Sicily. My grandfather was a fisherman and *his* grandfather was a fisherman. *I* was a fisherman in Sicily. All right, when I first came to America I worked on the railroad to make enough dollars to send for you, Rosa. But as soon as I can, I went back to the boats and to the sea. All the time the DiMaggios were fishermen. Now this one, your Giuseppe, all of a sudden to be a fisherman makes him sick? It's not possible. And I worry about that boy, Rosa."

He gulped the last of his coffee and got up from his chair. "So where's the boys?" he asked his wife.

"They'll be in soon, Papa. I let them sleep a little extra."

Giuseppe DiMaggio shook his head. In his day boys didn't expect to sleep a little extra when there was work to be done. "All right. I'll be down by the boat. Tell them to hurry up. The DiMaggios' boat is not the only one's gonna be out fishing today."

He took the lunch basket his wife handed him, then he kissed her gently on the cheek. "You better have a talk with that Giuseppe, Rosa," he said to her. "If not, he's gonna become a no-good loafer."

"Don't worry, Papa, he's gonna be all right," she said to him.

When her husband left, Rosalie DiMaggio busied herself with preparing breakfast for her boys. She sang softly as she set out the plates and the cups and saucers on the neat checkered cloth that covered the rectangular kitchen table. She thought of her little Giuseppe Paolo DiMaggio, named for his father, because she and her husband thought he would be the last child born to them. But God had blessed them with yet another, their ninth, a son Dominic.

What, indeed, would be with Giuseppe? What else could—or should—a DiMaggio be but a fisherman? Maybe, she thought guardedly—for her husband would frown at the idea—maybe if the fish run good and there is a little money Giuseppe and Vincent could finish school and become somebody. Not that being a fisherman was not a good thing, oh, no! But in America everyone does not have to be a fisherman.

"Good morning, Ma. Papa gone down to the boat already?" She was brought back to reality by Thomas, her oldest. He sat down at the table and watched hungrily as his mother put down a steaming bowl of cereal.

"Yes, Papa has gone. Where are your brothers?"

"Be in in a minute. They gotta grab that last minute's sleep. You know."

Mrs. DiMaggio nodded. She knew. And she understood now—not like Papa—that the iron discipline that parents of good Italian families in the old country expected was somehow not in keeping with things here. You were strict with your children in matters of respect and obedience, naturally. But—and she had so often discussed this with the other women at the market—the children born in America seem to be more independent. She wasn't sure this was such a good thing. Take Giuseppe, now. . . .

"Hi, Mama." It was Dominic, her baby, kissing her on the cheek before he sat down at the table.

She placed his bowl of cereal before him. "Dominic, you sure you want to go with your papa on the boat today? It's not easy work for a little boy like you."

"Sure, Mama," he answered eagerly. "I'm not a fraidy-cat like Joey. Am I, Vince?"

"Yeah, you're all right, Dom," his brother acknowledged.

"Dominic," his mother said sternly, but not too harshly, because he was her youngest and her favorite, "that's not nice to talk like that about your brother."

"Aw, Ma," Dominic retorted. "So what's he always layin' around in bed for whenever Papa wants us to go out with him? He's afraid he's going to drown or something, I'll bet."

"Lay off Joey for once, will you, guys?" Tom said. "If

he says he's sick, he's sick. You guys mind your own business. Joey's got enough keeping out of trouble with Pop, without you wiseguys starting up." He finished his breakfast and stood up. "C'mon, let's get going. Pop's waiting for us down at the docks."

The four youngsters chorused a "So long, Mom," and scooted out the door. Their mother walked to the front window and watched them until their figures were swallowed up by the darkness and the fog. Then she turned back to the kitchen and began clearing things away.

After a while she walked into her sons' bedroom. She leaned over and shook the small figure huddled in the big iron bed. "Giuseppe," she called firmly, "Giuseppe. Get up. Everybody's gone away. It's all right now."

3

The fog had completely disappeared and the sun was high by the time Giuseppe Paolo DiMaggio, Jr., walked out of the house on Taylor Street and set off for a leisurely tour of the neighborhood. His sisters Nellie, Mamie, Marie, and Frances were helping their mother with the housework. Later they would go down to the docks and wait for their father's return. They would see to the cleaning of the decks and would mend any nets that might have been torn by the day's catch.

But Giuseppe walked slowly down the hill toward Fisherman's Wharf, his hands in the pockets of the patched knickers that two years ago were his brother Vincent's, and he wondered what he might do that day to pass the time. One thing he knew, he'd better keep away from the docks during the afternoon, for if his father spotted him, he'd be dragged by his collar onto the boat to help clean up. And next to the fishing itself, what he hated most was cleaning the boat after a day out; it smelled of fish and salt, and the odor sickened him, even to think about it.

"Hey, Joey, wait up!" The call snapped him out of his lethargy. Across the street raced his friend Frank Venezia, with two other boys from the neighborhood.

"Where are you goin', Joe?" Frank asked him.

DiMaggio shrugged. "Just walking around. I don't know. Why, something doin'?"

"Yeah. We're gettin' up a game over at the Horse Lot. We could use a coupla more players. Come on."

Joe hesitated. "Aw, I don't know. I don't know if I feel like playing, Frankie."

"What's the matter, Joe?" Frank seemed astonished at his friend's refusal. "You gotta help your pop with the boat today or something?"

"No, you know I don't like to work with him on that boat. But I don't know, it's so hot and everything. Can't we find something else to do instead of playing baseball?"

"C'mon, willya, Joe?" his friend urged. "You'll never get to be like Babe Ruth that way."

"Who wants to be like Babe Ruth?" Joe returned. "You guys always talk like being a baseball player is such a big thing. My brother Tom could be one if he wanted to, but he don't even want to."

"C'mon, Joe," Frank pleaded. "Are we gonna stand here arguin' about your brother Tom or we gonna get a game goin'?"

DiMaggio thought a minute longer. "All right," he said finally. "I might as well. There's nothing else to do anyway."

The four youngsters walked on past the dock area until they came to a huge lot, jutted with rocks and patched with scrubgrass and clusters of purple-and-white clover.

Batting practice was already in progress while a dozen or so youngsters sprawled around on the grass, waiting for the two selected team leaders to choose up sides.

Joe DiMaggio, as usual in these sandlot pickup games, was sent to play third base, a position not without honor. Next to the shortstop, the third baseman is considered one of the most valuable men in a sandlot infield, since most young batters hit right-handed, to the left side of the infield.

He may not have approached these neighborhood games with enthusiasm, but once the action got under way, Joe pitched into it with all he had. Caught up in the excitement of the competition, he forgot his troubles at home, the fights with his father, the resentments of his brothers and sisters. The fishing boat could have been a thousand miles away for all he thought of it.

Joe fielded his third base well enough for a boy his age, but it was with a sawed-off oar-handled bat that he really won his place in the pickup games. He hit a line-drive single in the fourth inning. Then, in the eighth, with two teammates on base, he hit a towering drive that went over the left fielder's head and bounced off the foreleg of one of the startled horses.

Head down, Joe sped around the bases. He raced over the flat rock that served as second base, headed for the old potato sack that represented third.

"Slide, Joe, slide!" his teammates yelled. As he neared the base Joe flung himself in a headlong slide at the sack, reaching it with his fingertips safely ahead of the third baseman's tag. Joe picked himself up, spitting dirt, and dusted himself off. The heels of his hands were scraped raw from the slide, and one knee of his knickers hung torn, caught on the sharp pebbles that were embedded in the earth of the infield. But he was safe at third, and the cheers of his teammates made up for the bruises and the torn knickers.

When the game was over, the youngsters drifted away. Frank Venezia, Joe's best friend, George, and some of the other boys headed for the dock area at Fisherman's Wharf.

"Hey, you coming, Joe? We're gonna hang around the piers and watch 'em unload the fishing boats."

"No, not me. I'm gonna walk around a little, then I'm going home," Joe said.

Frank walked over to him. "Your pop's gonna be sore about the pants, eh, Joe?"

DiMaggio nodded. "And how. He don't like us to be playing baseball, especially me, you know. And stuff like this kills him. Every time we talk about playing baseball around the house, he yells, 'Too many shoes, too many pants.' Boy wait'll he sees what happened to these. I'll catch it."

"Yeah," Frank agreed soberly. "I pity you when you get home." He clapped Joe on the shoulder. "Well, I'm going with the guys. See you tonight maybe, after supper. Take it easy."

"Yeah, Frankie. You, too," Joe said. Then he turned away and walked slowly down the street in the opposite direction, away from the docks and the boats and the smell of fish.

Autumn came to San Francisco in a blaze of color, and the breeze from the sea had a new freshness. The nights turned cold. The sandlots and the schoolyards lost their little tenants with their tattered fielders' gloves and their patched-up baseballs. But on the weekends, and in the late afternoons when school was out, they began to return, wearing sweat shirts and woolen caps, to scrimmage on the pebbly lots. And the one who owned the football was elected captain of the team.

Not all of them returned, however. Papa DiMaggio had given up trying to make a fisherman out of the son to whom he had given his name. But enough was enough! A boy had to learn to work, now that he was twelve, and the family needed every penny it could earn.

So Joe DiMaggio was selling papers on the corner of Sutter and Sansone, in front of the Angelo Bank. Each afternoon, directly after school, he picked up his papers at the wholesalers and took his station at the bank, across the street from his younger brother Dominic.

"Paper? Paper, mister?" Joe knew he should be shouting it, but he said it quietly, half hoping the hurrying passers-by would ignore his offer. He could hear the shrill cry of Dominic hawking the headlines, and he saw that, as always, his brother was doing a brisk business.

Joe glanced up at the clock over the door of the bank. It was soon time to go home. He counted the papers he still had left. Fifteen! He'd never sell them at this rate, and Mr. Antonio, the wholesaler, would bawl him out plenty.

He wished he could be like Dom, yelling and hustling all over the place. But he hated to be conspicuous. He hated all jobs that kept him on the streets. He hated to be restricted. He wanted to feel free—to do anything he wanted. Mostly he wanted to be alone to do the things he liked, like tennis and sometimes playing baseball. He didn't like to go to school, for he felt embarrassed and humiliated when the teachers asked him questions and he could not answer correctly.

"Hey, Joey!" It was Dominic racing across the street. "I'm all sold out, Joey. How about you?" He looked at the papers under his brother's arm. "Gee, Joe, what you been doin' all afternoon? You hardly sold anything."

Joe shrugged. "I'm just not lucky, that's all, Dom. I'm not cut out to sell papers, anyway."

"Don't let Pop hear you say that. That's what you used to tell him about fishing, too. The only reason he stopped bothering you was because you told him you'd sell papers after school."

"So. Let him holler. I don't care. I'm gonna tell him. Maybe he'll let me quit school and get a job in a fruit market, like Vince did. I bet I could do that okay."

"You're supposed to go to high school next year, Joe. You know Mom wants us to graduate. She'll never let you quit."

"Sure she will. You'll see. Tom quit, didn't he? And Mike and Vince. And didn't Tom even have a chance to try out for third base with the Hollywood Stars? But he went to work for Pop on the boat. If I can get a good job Mom and Pop'll let me quit. You'll see."

Dom shook his head. "I don't know, Joey. Anyway, give me your papers. I'll sell some for you till we have to go home. Then Pop won't holler at you."

Dom took the papers from his brother Joe and began his brisk shouting, waving a folded paper in the air. By the time the boys turned for home, Dominic had sold them all for Joe.

The two brothers walked home slowly, Joe twelve

years old, Dominic nine, but both seemed older than their years with the bleak maturity that comes with being poor. It was growing dark now, the streetlamps suddenly came on, and the wind sweeping up the streets began to bite. Joe buttoned up his threadbare mackinaw, worn before him by Tom, then Mike, and then Vincent. Joe looked admiringly and with honest envy at Dominic's new mackinaw.

"Boy, you sure are lucky, Dom, getting a new lumberjacket. I always get Vinnie's stuff when it gets too small for him."

Dominic shrugged. "I guess Mom figured I couldn't wait till it got too small for you," he said, "so she bought me one instead."

"Well, I don't see why you should always be getting new things all the time. I never get any," Joe retorted. He didn't really resent his brother's good fortune, but he was angry at himself and his situation. The only way he could express his frustration was through resentment of his brother's new clothes.

As they turned up toward Taylor Street, they stopped in front of the neighborhood movie theater. They stared wide-eyed at the posters advertising *All Quiet on the Western Front*.

"Boy, it sure looks like a good picture," Dominic said.

"Yeah," Joe agreed. "I'll bet there's plenty of fighting in it. Boy, I sure wish we could see it."

They stood there looking longingly at the pictures and they could feel the weight of the coins in their pockets.

"Dom, you think if we ask Mom she'll let us go Saturday?" asked Joe. "It's only a dime apiece and we won't buy any candy."

"I don't know, Joe. Maybe she would if Pop goes out all day Saturday. I probably could talk her into it."

"Yeah, but maybe we better not. Mom don't have any extra money. We shouldn't ask her for money for the movies."

"Yeah, I guess you're right, Joe. We'll just have to miss that picture, I guess."

They continued up the hill, walking in silence, dreaming of the time they could go to the movies whenever they felt like it—and buy candy, too.

4

Frank Venezia, who was a boyhood pal of DiMaggio's, in talking about their school days together, said, "Joe really had a very good mind, but he just wasn't interested in school. Joe and I went to Hancock Grammar and Galileo High School. Hancock was in our own neighborhood with poor kids like us. But when we got to high school, it was different. Galileo High School was out of our neighborhood . . . it was completely different. There weren't many sons of fishermen there. The kids were from better sections of the city. They were much better dressed, they had better schooling and adjusted easily to the high-school life. It was a different world for Joe and me. It was a shock to us to see those kids in their new suits and ties, while we were wearing the same old shirts and pants we wore to school in our own neighborhood.

"Joe and I felt bad. We felt awkward and uncomfortable with the new kids and then one day when Joe was assigned to a new class . . . ROTC [Reserve Officers' Training Corps] when he wanted a new physical-education class . . . why, he just up and left school and didn't come back. That was the time he decided to talk to his folks about not continuing in school."

The living room of the DiMaggio home was quiet, ominously quiet. There was only the squeak of Papa DiMaggio's shoes as he paced the floor. There was no doubt about it, Papa DiMaggio was mad. Suddenly he wheeled about and faced his son Joe.

"I don't know what's gonna to be with this boy, Mama!" he shouted, his hands gesturing wildly in the air. He turned to his wife sitting, head bowed, on the faded blue sofa. "How many times I told you this boy's never gonna be no good! It's your fault, Rosa. I told you he should come with me on the boat, you said let him alone, Giuseppe, he's a sick boy, he's no got a stomach to be a fisherman.

"Okay," Mr. DiMaggio shrugged. "I leave him alone. You say let him go to school, Giuseppe, someday maybe he's gonna be somebody. I say okay, Mama, maybe you're right. Maybe he can be like you say, a bookkeeper. That's not so hard work, eh?—to go to school? And to be a book-keeper, you don't have to get up no four o'clock in the morning and work on a boat till ten o'clock at night, eh?

"So I listen to you, Rosa, and what happens?" He waved his hand at Joe. "Here's your boy, Rosa. He says he's not gonna be no fisherman. He's not gonna be no bookkeeper. He's not gonna go to school! He's fifteen years old and he's what you call it, a big shot already! He's the boss in the family!"

Papa DiMaggio resumed his angry pacing, muttering in Italian. He stopped again and spoke to his wife. "So,

Rosa. And you? You got nothing to say, eh? All of a sudden you got nothing to say, eh?"

Mrs. DiMaggio plucked absently at the worn fringes of the ancient sofa. "What can I tell you, Papa? You think it no hurts me, too, that Joe don't want to go to school? I wanted him to be somebody," she said feelingly. "Not a truck driver, or a dishwasher in a restaurant, not even a fisherman like you, Papa. He could make something from himself. He's got a chance to go to school and learn something good, to work with clean hands and make a good living. It hurts me, Papa. But what can we do?" She looked up at her son. "Joseph, you're sure you want to quit school? Maybe try a little more? Another year? You see, maybe you get to like it, eh?"

Joe shook his head. "Gee, Mom, I don't want you and Pop to think I don't appreciate your letting me finish high school if I want to. But I just don't like school, that's all. I can't be a bookkeeper or anything like that. That takes a lot of schooling. Why waste my time? I could be out making money working someplace instead of wasting my time hanging around in school not learning anything."

Mr. DiMaggio gestured to his wife. "Hah, you see, Mama? You talk to this boy, it's like talking to a piece of wood. You want to go out and work, eh, Giuseppe?" he said to his son. "What are you gonna do? You got a job somebody wants to give you?"

"Please call me Joe, Pop," Joe said. "Sure, I got a job all set. I'm gonna sell papers full time, that's all. Instead of just hanging around the corner, I figure I'll try to build up a little route. Lots of guys do that. They make out pretty good, too."

Mr. DiMaggio nodded his head disgustedly. "That's a

good trade, selling newspapers. Someday maybe you're gonna own your newspaper stand, eh?"

"Aw, Pop," Joe said. "I won't always sell papers. When I'm older maybe I'll try a trade or something. Right now I just want to get out and work, and help with the money, that's all. Besides, we sure could use the money home."

Mr. DiMaggio looked at his wife. She shrugged helplessly. He shrugged, too. "Okay, Rosa. I wash my hands with the boy. If he's ever gonna be somebody, I'm gonna be the most surprised man in the whole United States."

Joe ran true to his father's predictions. With little education and no particular skills, he sold papers. He tried squeezing oranges at a soft-drink stand. That lasted one day. He was a grocery delivery boy for a couple of weeks, then an odd job here and there, then back to the newspaper route again.

In the spring of 1931, when Joe was sixteen, a buzz of excitement ran through the neighborhood. A man named Joe Rossi, owner of the Rossi Olive Oil Company, was willing to sponsor a neighborhood baseball club in the Class B sandlot league in San Francisco. In return for buying the uniforms and equipment, he got the name of his olive-oil company spelled out on the front of the uniforms.

The nucleus of the team was made up of the same boys who had been playing together for years on the old Horse Lot near Fisherman's Wharf. Frank Venezia, Joe's old friend and buddy on the newspaper route, was captain of the team, and was chosen to recruit Joe for the third-base job. There were, however, two major problems.

For one thing, Frank and Joe hadn't spoken to each other for a year. Once best friends, they had argued with each other the year before over their newspaper-selling business and parted bitter enemies. The other problem was that Joe wasn't excited about playing baseball at all. He had become interested instead in the careers of two top tennis players from San Francisco, Bill Johnston and Maurice McLoughlin, and decided that tennis was his game. He borrowed a racket wherever he could and played on makeshift courts in neighborhood parks and schoolyards. He was getting pretty good at it, too, when Frank Venezia brought him back to baseball.

When Venezia first knocked on Joe's door, DiMaggio didn't know what to make of it.

"What's up, Venezia?" he asked suspiciously.

"Uh, can I come in a minute, Joe? I got something pretty important to talk to you about."

DiMaggio hesitated a moment. Then he swung the door open. "Okay, come on in." His curiosity was aroused.

He indicated the couch for his friend and settled into an armchair himself. "So what's the story?" he said.

"Um, listen, Joe, you know this guy Rossi, he owns the olive-oil company near here?" DiMaggio shrugged.

"Well, he wants us guys to get up a team and get into the regular sandlot league. He's gonna give us the uniforms, the bats and the balls, and everything we need. Like a regular team, the works, you know? And the guys we always played with, we're getting together. And well, they asked me to come over and get you to join up. With you, I just know we can win the crown."

Joe was genuinely flattered, but he wasn't so sure he wanted to play. "I don't know, Frank," he said. "I don't think it's for me. Anyway, why's this guy Rossi handing out all that money for a team for us?"

Venezia spread his hands wide. "What do we care why? It's a terrific deal for us, Joe. He wants to spend the money, let him spend it. Maybe he's just a nice guy. Maybe it's good advertising for his store. He gets his name on the uniforms, and the people in the neighborhood figure he's a great guy giving us uniforms and everything —and they buy his olive oil.

"But listen, Joe. I mean let's forget about you and me being sore at each other and everything. This team could be a lot of fun, gosh, with uniforms and everything. How about it, huh? We ain't never had uniforms before."

"Aw, I really don't know, Frank. It's not because we're sore at each other or anything like that. I just don't feel like baseball's such a big thing, that's all."

"But gee, Joe," his friend persisted. "We're counting on you for third base. You're the best guy around here on third. And you know you can hit good, too. We really need you."

Joe really wasn't interested in taking up baseball again, but he felt obligated to join the team. Besides, his friends might call him a sorehead for not joining, because of his fight with Frank Venezia the year before.

Joe sighed resignedly. "I guess okay, Frank. Count me in for third. I wouldn't want to let you guys down. When do we get together?"

"Atta boy, Joe!" Frank was jubilant. "We're meeting Saturday morning at nine o'clock at the Horse Lot. Then we got to go over to Rossi's place and meet him. And listen, Joe, let's shake hands on this thing, eh? Be friends again?"

"Okay, Frankie," Joe agreed. He got up and shook his

friend's hand as he walked him to the door. "But between
you and me I don't think much of this whole thing."

So Joe DiMaggio went to third base for the Rossi Olive
Oil Company baseball team. And it would be twenty
years or more before he would put his glove away again
for good.

5

For once in his life, Papa DiMaggio had to admit he might have been wrong. It would never do to say so out loud, to his family. That would be bad for discipline. Still, he was forced to acknowledge the fact that this crazy game of baseball he had been scorning for years might have something to it after all. Here was his son Vincent, standing in front of him now, telling him a big baseball team was going to pay him big money to play with them!

"Tell me again, Vincenzio," Mr. DiMaggio said. "How much you say these people gonna pay you?"

Vince grinned. "A hundred and fifty dollars a month, Pop."

Mr. DiMaggio shook his head in disbelief. In 1932 that was a considerable amount of money for an ordinary wage earner. "And all you gotta do for this money is play baseball every day? Play games for all that money?"

Vince nodded. "Every day during the regular season. I hope, anyway."

Mr. DiMaggio still looked puzzled. "Maybe I don't understand. You mean all you gotta do every day is play baseball. When you finish you come home and do nothing. And for this, every month they gonna pay you a hundred and fifty dollars? This America. She is a funny place. All that money for a game."

"That's right, Pop."

Mr. DiMaggio shrugged his shoulders. "That's a crazy business, if you ask me. You sure you can trust these people, Vincenzio? They're not gonna fool you? You got this on a paper?"

Vince laughed. "Pop, this is a big team, known all around the country. It's the San Francisco Seals. It's just one step away from the major leagues. If I make good and move up to the major leagues I'll really make big money."

"Well, if you say it's all right, I guess you know what you're doing," Mr. DiMaggio said. "When you gotta start this business?"

"Well, I'm not going to be playing San Francisco right away, Pop. First they're sending me out to their farm team in Tucson, Arizona. I got to report there next week."

That night Mama DiMaggio cooked a big spaghetti dinner in honor of her son's big news. If her eyes appeared wet through the cloud of steam from the huge bowl of spaghetti, well, maybe it was the onions she peeled for the sauce. In the midst of such merriment, there was no room for tears; she felt, however, that she was losing her son Vincent to a city with the strange name of Tucson.

The DiMaggio children were bubbling over with happiness and pride. Vincent, their brother, was going to be a professional baseball player! And not one of them doubted that before long he would be hastening East to play with the major leagues. Tom, the eldest, was a little

wistful as he congratulated Vince. He had been a standout third baseman, and the Hollywood club had given
him a tryout. But Tom had felt he was needed at home to
help in the fishing business.

"Gee, Tom," Vince was saying to him now, "it's too bad
you couldn't take that crack at Hollywood that time.
You'd have made it easy. Maybe we'd be playing on the
same team someday."

"I don't know, Vince," Tom said. "My arm went bad on
me and I probably wouldn't have stuck in Hollywood. Besides, one of us had to help Papa full time. I guess it's me.
I'm not kicking."

"Well, it's too bad. You could have been one of the
greatest. Eh, Joe?"

Joe shrugged. He was only half listening to the conversation at the table. Vince's signing with San Francisco
had set him to some serious thinking. He had done well
with the Rossi baseball team the year before, hitting two
home runs in the playoff game for the league championship. This year, the same team, virtually intact, was
moving up to some faster company in the Sunset Produce
League. Joe was still not enthusiastic about baseball as a
sport, but this business of Vince, now this changed the
picture somewhat. He could do the same thing as Vince.
Besides, he was a better ballplayer. Might he make more
than Vince?

Ignoring the buzz of excited conversation around the
dinner table, Joe began to steer a course for himself. In
his mind he ran down a list of the fellows he knew around
the neighborhood. Most of them were out of work, or
doing odd jobs, going from place to place, no future, no
money. Like himself, he admitted they were all failures.

Now here was Vince getting good money, with a terrific future ahead of him, and all for playing baseball.

If Vince can do it, I can do it, Joe thought grimly. There's good money being paid to play baseball and I'm going to get some of it. It seems to run in the family, anyhow. Tom could have done it. Vince is doing it. Well, me, I'm next. How I'm going to break in I don't know, maybe Vince can help when he gets settled down.

But there's one thing I'm sure of, Joe promised himself, from now on I'm not just fooling around out there. Baseball's my game from now on. I'm gonna be real serious about it, now.

"Hey, Joe, wake up!" Vince was laughing across the table. "What are you doing, dreaming where your first million's coming from? I asked you three times how your team figures to do in this new Sunset Produce League."

"No, I was just thinking of something, Vince. I guess we'll do all right. The guys in this league aren't very different from the Boys' Club League. And we won the championship there, remember?"

"Yeah," Vince said. "And I remember what you got for knocking their brains out with your hitting. Two gold baseballs and about eight dollars' worth of merchandise? I told you, Joe, you stop fooling around and play this game with everything you got and it'll be worth your while. Look at me. I'm not the greatest player in the world, but I'm going to make a good business out of this game, and I like it fine. Can you beat that?"

Joe responded with his usual shrug. "Maybe it's a good deal, maybe it's not so good. I don't know, Vince."

But in his heart, Joe knew. For the first time in his life, he knew what he wanted.

He fell into an exhausted sleep finally, and when his father passed by his room in the gray dawn, Papa DiMaggio wondered at the sounds that came from the sleeping figure of his son. "That's a funny boy," Papa DiMaggio muttered sadly. "I don't know what's gonna be with him."

6

Fred Hoffman, seasoned manager of the San Francisco Missions of the Pacific Coast League, sat behind his desk in his office under the stands and appraised the skinny young ballplayer standing in front of him. His scouts had reported that Joe DiMaggio was a strong, though scattered-armed, third baseman and shortstop. But he could hit like a seasoned star. DiMaggio had, in fact, hit .632 in eighteen games for the Sunset Produce team that season, winning a valuable pair of lightweight baseball shoes as the outstanding player in the local Class A League.

"DiMaggio," Hoffman said to Joe, "I've been getting some nice reports about you from my sandlot scouts. They tell me you really were the best in the league this year."

Joe shrugged modestly. "I didn't do bad, I guess."

"Well, I don't want to beat around the bush with you. I'd like you to work out the rest of this season with the Missions. If you look good, I'll sign you on. Hundred and fifty a month."

Joe didn't move a muscle, but his brain began to whirl. Just like that, a professional offer, and for a hundred and fifty a month! If I'm that good, Joe thought. . . .

"I tell you, Mr. Hoffman," he told the Missions' manager, "the offer sounds okay to me. But I don't know too much about these things, so I think I better talk it over with my brother Tom first before signing. Okay with you?"

Hoffman smiled wryly. "What's the matter, DiMaggio, isn't the money good enough? Hundred and fifty a month is a lot of dough these days. Lots of men with families don't make what I'm offering you."

"Oh, it's not that at all, Mr. Hoffman. But Tom is the oldest in the family, and he's kind of like the business manager for everybody. And like I said, I don't know anything about contracts, so I want Tom to know about it before I give my word on it. That's all."

"Okay, DiMaggio. I guess that's only sensible. Let me know soon as you make up your mind."

Before Joe had a chance to discuss the offer with Tom, however, his future was decided by a knothole in a ballpark fence.

While Joe was clouting the pitching in his Class A League games on Sunday, brother Vince was doing the same every day at Tucson. He was batting .347 and leading the league in home runs when the Seals recalled him to San Francisco. Joe, in between jobs at the time, used to wander around to the park every day to watch Vince play.

Joe couldn't afford the price of a ticket, and he was too shy to ask for a pass on the strength of being a brother of one of the Seals' players. So he used to take up a post at the fence near the players' entrance, where there was a knothole strategically situated for a good view of the ball game.

One afternoon Joe was looking through the knothole,

rooting for Vince and the Seals, when he felt a hand on his shoulder. His heart skipped with fright. Was it a park policeman?

Joe turned slowly and was relieved to see that it was not a policeman, but a smiling-faced man who appeared somewhat familiar.

"You're Vince DiMaggio's brother, aren't you, kid?" the man asked.

"That's right. How'd you know?"

"I'm Spike Hennessy, the scout for the Seals, here. I've seen you around the sandlots. You did all right with that Sunset team, too."

"Listen, Mr. Hennessy," Joe pleaded, "you don't care if I watch the games through this hole, do you?"

Hennessy laughed. "Heck, no. But listen, kid, I always say never stand on the outside looking in. Come on with me." He took Joe by the arm.

"Like I said, we're going inside. I'll introduce you to Charley Graham. He owns the Seals."

"I-I-I don't want to go in. What do I want to meet Mr. Graham for? He's liable to be sore if you tell him I've been peeking in at the games."

"Come on, come on," Hennessy assured Joe, practically dragging him through the entrance. "Nobody's gonna eat you up."

Hennessy guided the scared young DiMaggio down the dark hallways under the stands to Graham's office. "Here's DiMaggio's kid brother," the scout said to the president of the Seals. "I found him watching the game through that old knothole by the players' entrance."

Graham stuck out his hand to shake Joe's. "Glad to meet you, young fellow," he said. "Why didn't you come around and see me before? No need to go peeking in through knotholes. Here," he said, reaching into his desk drawer. "Here's a bunch of passes for you. When you run out, come around and I'll see you get some more."

"Well, gee, that's darn nice of you, Mr. Graham," Joe stuttered his thanks.

"Tell me something, son," Graham went on. "Vince do all the ball playing in your family, or do you do some yourself?"

"Well, I—" Joe started, but Hennessy interrupted him.

"Does he do any playing himself, you ask?" he said to Graham. "I've been keeping a good eye on this lad, Charley, and I'll say he does a bit of playing for himself. Maybe you don't remember, but I've dropped his name around the office here a couple of times. He's got a good, strong arm for a shortstop, a bit wild, but we'll work on that, and he's got a swing that's as smooth as anything I've ever seen in baseball."

Graham waved his hand at Hennessy. "Whoa, Spike, whoa! You his agent or something? I remember you mentioning his name, all right. I just wanted to see what the boy had to say for himself." He turned to Joe. "You interested in trying out with us, son?"

Joe was even more confused than when the Missions had made him an offer. He knew that baseball scouts sometimes watched the sandlot games, but he never realized they had been keeping such a close eye on him for so long. He mentally brushed aside the offer from the Missions. In an instant he decided. The Seals were his brother Vince's team; therefore it was his, too.

"I'd love to work out with the Seals, Mr. Graham," he blurted out finally. "I'm not working now, and I could start in right away, today."

Graham nodded approval. "The season's almost over,

anyway. No matter what—we're not going any higher than sixth place. You can't hurt us any if we decide to use you in a game, and the experience won't hurt you any, either. Come in tomorrow morning and report to Manager Ike Caveney. Meantime I'll tell him to expect you." Graham stood up and extended his hand. "Good luck, son. Keep your wits about you."

For the first few days, working out with the Seals meant little more than hanging around during practice, getting to hit a few in the batter's cage, shagging flies in the outfield, getting an occasional chance at infield workouts. Joe didn't even get a Seals' uniform. He wore his new spiked shoes that he won with the Sunset Produce team, and his Sunset uniform. He was beginning to despair of getting into even one game before the season ended, when suddenly he got his break at last.

With only a Saturday game and a Sunday doubleheader left to end the season, outfielder Henry Oana asked to be let off so that he could go home to Hawaii. Augie Galan, then the Seals' shortstop, asked if he could join Oana for a vacation. Manager Caveney agreed, since it would make no difference in the Seals' fortunes that season.

Friday afternoon, however, after Galan and Oana had departed, Caveney suddenly burst into the Seals' locker room. "Hey!" he yelled to the dressing ballplayers. "I just thought of something! I got nobody to play shortstop tomorrow and Sunday!"

Vince DiMaggio, who was at the door, just ready to leave, heard the manager's cry. "Say, Ike, how about my kid brother Joe? He's been working out with us for a few days. And he's a shortstop."

Caveney shouted at Vince. "Is he any good? Don't kid me, Vince. We're not going anywhere and he don't have to be no Frankie Crosetti or anything. But I don't want to look like a darn fool with this kid brother of yours out there."

Vince grinned. "He's liable to show you a couple of things, Ike. Don't worry, he's not going to embarrass anybody but maybe a couple of pitchers."

"Okay, Vince," the manager agreed. "I guess I'm stuck with him. Tell your kid brother to get in here extra early tomorrow."

Joe was so excited when Vince told him the news he couldn't eat his dinner. Later that night, as he lay in his darkened room, he broke out in a cold sweat thinking about what he faced the next day. This was his big chance. He had three games to play with a real professional baseball team. Three games to show them what he could do.

He twisted and turned as thoughts of glory and failure raced through his mind. One moment he imagined himself the hero of a game, driving in the winning runs with a tremendous home run in the ninth inning, or saving the day with a great stop that turned a sure hit into a game-ending double play. Then he groaned aloud as he saw himself letting a simple ground ball trickle through his legs as the winning runs scampered across the plate, the enemy players laughing at him and hooting from the bench.

7

The locker room of the San Francisco Seals was loud with the easy chatter of the dressing ballplayers. With the season only two days from being over, and no change in standing involved in the final games, the Seals were a relaxed group. There was one in their midst, however, a tall, sallow-faced, thin-shouldered youth, whose frozen features and glum reticence betrayed his anxiety.

For Joe DiMaggio was really scared. He stood in front of his locker, nervous and embarrassed, watching out of the corner of his eye as the other players dressed. He didn't even know how to put on his sliding pads, an item of luxury equipment he never owned in his sandlot playing days. He got them on finally after furtively watching a nearby player slip his pads into place; hoping fervently that no one had noticed his clumsiness and ignorance.

He pulled on his baseball pants, and then watched carefully as a player at the end of the row of lockers rolled the bottoms below the knee, and he rolled his own likewise. He wished that his brother Vince was nearby to help him. But then he was glad Vince wasn't, for to have asked his brother would have added to his embarrassment.

Several of the San Francisco players nodded in friendly fashion or smiled a "Hiya" to Joe. He was so tense, he could barely nod back. His lips were set in tight lines. At last he walked out of the locker room and up the steps of the dugout to the playing field. He blinked in the bright sunlight, but he felt a little better away from the confining walls of the stuffy room, away from the curious glances of the veteran Seals.

He walked over to the batting cage and watched the rival team, the San Francisco Missions, take their practice swings. Next to him, watching, too, were several of Joe's new teammates. One of them turned to him.

"Hey, you're Vince DiMaggio's kid brother, aren't you?"

Joe just nodded dumbly.

"You're the guy taking Galan's place at short today, eh?"

DiMaggio nodded again.

The player looked at him for a long moment. Then he shrugged. He turned to the veteran players at his side. "Friendly guy, ain't he?" he said.

Joe took his turn in the batting cage in a kind of trance. He almost prayed he'd fall and hurt himself, or be hit by a ball and knocked unconscious—anything to avoid the inevitable moment when he'd have to go out there and play his first professional game.

Finally the batting cage was rolled away. And Joe DiMaggio, seventeen years old, his knees turning to water and his heart in his throat, trotted out to his position at shortstop.

At DiMaggio's right, playing third base for the Seals, was the experienced former Yankee, Jules Wera. "Just play it loose, kid," Wera advised Joe as they waited for the Seals' hurler to come down with the first pitch of the game.

In the second inning Joe saw his first action. The Missions' batter slapped a half-speed grounder to DiMaggio. Joe dove for the ball, came up with it cleanly, but was afraid he would throw the ball over the first baseman's head if he cut loose. So he merely lobbed the ball to first, barely catching the runner by a half step.

At third base, the veteran Wera let out a bellow that could have been heard around the ball park.

"You dumb busher. Wing that ball!"

By the second inning some of Joe's nervousness was wearing off. He waited at the on-deck spot for his turn to hit. As scared as he was, he really felt he could hit this pitching.

Now he had his chance. On the mound for the Missions was Ted Pillette, a smart curve-ball pitcher who had played for several big-league teams. Pillette sized up the slim rookie as DiMaggio strode into the hitter's box. Joe squared his shoulders and dug his spikes into the dirt. His hawkish features were set with determination.

Pillette picked up the sign from his batterymate, took a full windup, and spun a big sweeping curve ball that caught the corner of the plate. The umpire's right hand shot up.

"Strike one!"

Joe set himself easily in the box, his feet wide apart, and waved his bat back and forth a couple of times waiting for the next pitch from Pillette. The ball came in tight and high, a fast ball. DiMaggio leaned back and took it for ball one.

Pillette tried again with his big curve. As the pitch

broke toward the outside corner Joe whipped his bat around in a blurring arc and sent the ball soaring deep into left field. DiMaggio tore down the first-base line, the roar of the crowd in his ears. As he rounded the bag he saw the left fielder leap in vain against the barrier as the ball kicked off the wall and ricocheted back toward the infield.

Head down, Joe raced for second, tore around the base, stumbled as his foot caught the sack, regained his balance, and scampered for third. He was running almost blindly in his excitement, like a rank sandlotter, forgetting to watch the coach at third base. He did notice the third baseman straddling the bag, waiting for the throw-in, and he threw himself into a headlong slide, reaching with his fingertips for the safety of the third-base sack.

He was safe at third; had hit a tremendous triple in his first time at bat as a professional baseball player! But as he stood up grinning happily and slapping the dust off his uniform, he saw only the glowering face of the third-base coach.

"Didn't you see me holding my hands up, kid? You didn't have to slide to make it. Next time keep your eyes on me instead of charging around the bags like a wild elephant."

Joe bit his lip. But even the crushing knowledge that he had indeed run the bases like an amateur could not dull entirely his satisfaction at the hit.

Joe accepted silently the words of praise from his teammates when he ran into the dugout after scoring a few moments later. But in the fourth inning, he could have used a few of those kind words.

With one out, Joe's second fielding chance came his

way. He scooped up a hard ground ball, but remembering third baseman Wera's jeer at his first throw, Joe put everything he had into this one. And just as he had feared, the ball went sailing high over the first baseman's leaping stretch. The wild throw carried all the way into the grandstand seats behind first base. Joe scuffed at the ground disgustedly as the runner trotted into second, grinning.

"That's quite an arm you got there, kid," Wera called to Joe. "They better stick you in the outfield, though, before you kill somebody."

DiMaggio got through the remainder of the game without any repetition of wild throwing. In the fifth inning he grounded out. In the eighth he sent the center fielder back to the wall to pull down a line drive.

After his initial fielding jitters were over, Joe settled down to an errorless, if not particularly inspired, game of shortstop. He was credited with seven assists and four putouts, winding up with a .917 fielding average.

The final game of the season over, the players dressed quietly in the locker room. It had been a poor season. The Seals finished in sixth place. Now the players talked about what they would do until training got under way again the following spring. Unlike major-league players, few of the Seals talked about long vacations, of fishing and hunting trips. They were low-salaried men. They were paid in the Pacific Coast League at a monthly salary, on a six-month-season basis. So the talk was of the jobs they were going back to—as salesmen, as factory hands.

Joe was combing his smooth black hair, stooping to look into the mirror on the door of the locker, when Manager Ike Caveney walked up to him. "DiMaggio, drop around to the office tomorrow morning, will you? The boss'd like to have a little talk with you. Okay?"

Joe gulped, nodded. "Sure thing, Mr. Caveney. I'll be there, all right."

Caveney grunted and turned back to his other players, shaking hands, telling them good-bye.

His heart thumping, Joe finished dressing. He could hardly wait to get outside and tell Vince. Caveney and Graham wanted to talk to him! It could only mean that they wanted to sign him for next year. Then a sudden doubt hit him. Maybe not! Maybe they just wanted to tell him he didn't have it, wasn't good enough for the Seals.

But how could that be? Didn't he get a triple and a double? Didn't he prove he could hit the pitching in this league? He winced as he thought of his fielding in the first game. They'll know I was just nervous, he thought. They've handled rookies before.

Doubts and questions filled his mind now. If Caveney was just going to drop him, why go to the trouble of making him come to the office tomorrow? Why not tell him now? Well, he concluded, maybe he didn't want to embarrass me in front of the other guys. Maybe he just wants to let me down easy, give me a pep talk and all that.

Joe shook his head to clear his mind. He didn't know what to think anymore. He was right back where he had started two days before. He was scared. Just plain scared.

The very next morning, bright and early Joe walked into the offices of the San Francisco Seals convinced he was going to get a fatherly lecture and a polite invitation to go back to the sandlots. As he stood in front of the desk of Charley Graham, the Seals' president, he felt as if he were facing the hangman. The smile of Manager Ike Caveney, who was half sitting on the window ledge behind Graham, seemed sad and sympathetic, a portent of Joe's doom.

Graham, shuffling idly through a sheaf of papers on his desk, finally looked up at Joe. He cleared his throat. "Sit down, DiMaggio," he said indicating a worn red leather armchair against the wall.

"Now then," he continued, "let's figure out what we're going to do with this boy." He swung his chair around to face the manager. "Ike, what do you think?"

Caveney seemed to hesitate for a moment. Graham addressed him again. "Come on, Ike, I want your opinion, right here, in front of this boy. That's why I wanted you here with me. I don't want Joe to think we just pick a few names out of a hat and the lucky boys make it and the unlucky ones don't. Whatever we decide here today, I want him to know why we decided it."

Caveney nodded. He knew Graham had already made up his mind about DiMaggio. So had he, for that matter, and both men had discussed DiMaggio's future with the Seals at some length the evening before. But this way was best. DiMaggio, they had recognized, was a very sensitive young man, sure of himself on the ball field, but terribly aware of his immaturity, his background, and his ignorance except where baseball was concerned.

If he were not handled properly now, he would crawl deeper into his shell. He might quit baseball altogether. Caveney knew how to handle kids. They were insecure, frustrated, and unless you handled them just right, you could affect their lives forever.

"Well, I'll tell you now, Mr. Graham," Caveney said at

last. "You know I'm high on Joe here. I think he's going to be all right. He hits the ball with real power, fast on the bases, can handle himself in the field. Someday he's going to have those major-league scouts fall all over themselves trying to get him away from us.

"But there's a couple of things got to be smoothed out yet. The way he plays that shortstop now. It just isn't safe for a person to sit along the first-base line during the game. Joe here's liable to brain them with one of his throws. But we can correct that with practice."

DiMaggio winced at the truth of this, but Manager Caveney was smiling when he said it, in order to soften the criticism. Graham smiled, "What do you think of Ike's opinion, DiMaggio? You can speak right up. You think Ike's been fair, or is he all wet?"

Joe looked down at his shoes. "He's right, I guess," he said without raising his head. Then he looked up, his face somberly determined. "But I can hit the pitching in this league, Mr. Graham. That's one thing I know I can do. And I can learn to play shortstop. My arm's strong, you can see that. I just gotta learn to control it, that's all."

Graham smiled tolerantly at DiMaggio's outburst. "That's all," he repeated. He sat there for a minute, drumming his fingers on the desk. "So you think you can make good with the Seals?" he said at last.

DiMaggio fidgeted in his chair. He didn't want to appear boastful. But how could you say no to a question like that? Especially when no isn't what you really felt. "Yes, I do, Mr. Graham," he said. "I just know it, sir. All I want is the chance."

"And you think you'd like to make the Seals your team? I understand the Missions have made you an offer."

"Yes, they have. But, you know, since my brother Vince

has been with your club I've always felt kind of like they were my team, you know what I mean. If I can, I'd like to play with them. With you, that is."

Graham nodded. "Tell you what, DiMaggio," he said thoughtfully. "You know, we got a special training school down at the spring-training camp that we open before regular training starts, so that we can give a good workout to promising youngsters like you. By the way, how old are you, DiMaggio?"

"I'll be eighteen November 25."

"Good. Well, as I was saying," Graham went on, "how'd you like to come down next spring and work out at our baseball school?"

Joe sat silent a moment. He felt curiously elated and disappointed at the same time. His worst fear—that he was to be dropped entirely—had been eliminated. He was to be given a chance. Still, what he had scarcely dared dream, but had hoped for anyway, had been denied him too. He hadn't been given a contract. He hadn't definitely made it with the Seals. He would just be another green busher trying to latch on next season. Considering the fact that he had actually played three games during the regular season, and not too badly at that, he was disappointed. Well, at least he was to get another crack at making it.

"What do you say?" Graham interrupted his thoughts. "It's up to you, DiMaggio. We'd like to have you down there for a look. We'll pay all your expenses, and if you look good we'll talk contract. But if you'd rather not, you needn't feel obligated. Maybe you'd like to try another club. . . ."

"Oh, no, Mr. Graham," Joe assured the Seals' president.

"It's not that at all. I, uh . . . I'll be glad to come down to the school. I guess I just didn't know what to expect and I'm a little excited. But I'd really like to come down."

"Okay, then," Graham stood up, indicating the meeting was over. "We'll be sending you a letter telling you when and where to report." He stuck his hand out and shook DiMaggio's. "Good luck, boy. Keep in shape and work on that long throw from short. It's all-important for a good shortstop."

"I will, Mr. Graham," Joe promised. "And thanks a lot. You, too, Mr. Caveney. Thanks."

"Sure thing, Joe," Caveney said. "See you next spring."

When the door closed behind the youngster, Caveney turned to Graham.

"Someday, Charley, that kid's going to break a few records around this league. Or my name's not Ike Caveney."

Graham nodded. "Your name," he said soberly, "is indeed Ike Caveney."

Joe's return home was awaited eagerly by his brothers and sisters. The prospect of having two ballplayers in the family was an exciting one, except to Papa DiMaggio. One boy in the house playing the silly game of baseball for a living was enough, money or no money. But two baseball players! As far as Papa was concerned, it was a shame upon the name of DiMaggio. He would be the laughingstock of all the other fishermen.

During dinner, Joe had to recount for everyone exactly what Manager Caveney and Graham had said, and what he said and what they said again. "Don't worry, Joe," Vince said. "Caveney's been watching you. If he didn't think you'd make it next year he wouldn't have let Graham tell you to come back."

"Why didn't they sign me, then?" Joe retorted, seeking more encouragement from Vince.

"Graham just don't work that fast," Vince soothed. "Before he shells out good dough he wants to be darn sure he's gonna get his money's worth, that's all. After all, you only played three games, and at the end of the season when nobody was really trying as hard as they might have at the beginning. Maybe he figures your hits were flukes, or something. But like I said, if they weren't pretty sure you'd make it next year, they wouldn't have bothered telling you to come down. I know how Caveney works, Joe."

Joe's father, following the conversation, broke in suddenly. "How much they gonna pay you, Giuseppe, to play this game? Same like Vincent?"

"I don't know exactly, Pop. We didn't settle that."

"You no sign yet a paper, how you say it, Vincent?" He turned to his other son.

"A contract, Pop," Vince said.

"*Sì*. A contract. You no sign this yet, Giuseppe?"

Vince tried to answer the question. "You see, Pop, they want Joe to come down to the training camp next spring—"

"I ask Giuseppe, not you," his father stopped him.

Joe swallowed. "No, Pop."

"So why you gonna play? You gonna get another pair of shoes with pins sticking out like before?"

In spite of his anxiety, Joe grinned at his father's description of the spiked shoes he had won with the Sunset Produce team. "No, Pop. Let me explain. I didn't get a contract *yet*. But I'm sure I will after spring training next year. They just want to look me over again before signing me up."

"And what if they look you over and they say 'Go home'?"

Joe shrugged. "So I go home."

His father nodded. "If I'm you I stay home in the first place. You gonna save everybody a lot of trouble."

Vince wound a portion of spaghetti expertly around his fork and interjected, "You'd be surprised, Pop. Joe's a darn good baseball player. He's gonna make the team all right next year. You should have come out Saturday or Sunday and watched him play. You might have enjoyed it."

Papa DiMaggio snorted. "Baseball! A crazy game! You hit a ball with a stick and a whole bunch of crazy fellas in short pants run around like crazy fools. *Bocci.* That's a good game," he said, referring to a traditional Italian game, something like lawn bowling, played by the older men in the neighborhood.

In disgust, Mr. DiMaggio got up from the dinner table and went to his room. His attitude had dulled the excitement of the evening, and the DiMaggios continued their meal in silence. Finally Vince spoke again. "Aw, you know Pop by now, Joe. You make the team next year and he'll come around." But he failed to raise his brother's dampened spirits.

Joe rose, his meal unfinished, and walked out of the house. He turned automatically down Taylor Street, heading for Fisherman's Wharf. It was nearly dusk, and the sky in the east was already turning inky blue, the clouds purple underneath, and red, too, where they caught the reflecting rays of the sinking sun.

Joe wandered along the waterfront. He walked to the end of one of the piers and stood for a moment, gazing out to sea. The breeze was coming in fresh and salty, and Joe sat down at the edge of the pier, his feet dangling over the side. He just sat, thinking, and looked out over the vast expanse of black water, hearing, without listening, the soft lapping of the tide against the wooden pilings below him.

After a while his brother Tom joined him. They sat, neither speaking, letting the silence communicate the warmth of their feelings for each other. At that moment, the two brothers, far apart in years, were perhaps closer than they had ever been before.

The sun died a fiery death, the lights came on along the waterfront, and they could make out the sweep of the searchlights from the towers of Alcatraz. Tom took out a cigarette and lit it, and the match was like a torch in the night.

"You know something, Joe," he said at last, "don't feel too bad at not getting a contract. Everybody was talking about your play in those three games. I'll bet you go with the Seals next year."

"Gee, Tom, wouldn't that be great!" said the excited Joe. "Me a regular player with the Seals."

"More than that, Joe. You've got a better batting eye than Vince, and I got a hunch you'll be up there with one of the big-league teams in a couple of years."

"I don't know about the majors, Tom. I'll be satisfied to make the Seals next year. They're plenty good."

"Joe, listen to me. You really bear down, get serious about baseball. Concentrate on your batting. The big leagues want batters. You just keep on hitting—and take the game serious. You've got a great arm, plenty fast on the bases. You've got all the makings."

Joe turned to him surprised, and even in the darkness Tom could see the gratitude glistening in his kid brother's eyes.

"You just wait and see, Tom. Just wait and see."

8

The Seals' 1933 training camp was crowded with 150 youngsters of all sizes, ages, and abilities. None, however, carried more potential than Joe DiMaggio. And probably none was more nervous than Joe. From the day he arrived at camp, Manager Ike Caveney, who had been a standout shortstop with the Cincinnati Reds, worked with him at the position. But to little avail.

When Joe reported to the Seals' training camp he was a tall stringbean of a kid. Almost overnight he began to fill out and put on weight. "I was trying to become an infielder then," Joe said, frankly, "and I was terrible. I think it was Charley Graham who said that I was the clumsiest ballplayer he had ever seen. He was probably right."

Joe couldn't seem to get the fluidity into his fielding so necessary to a shortstop. Though he managed to field balls hit his way and throw runners out, it soon became apparent to Manager Caveney that the infield was never going to be Joe's position. Aside from his fielding, Joe couldn't make those quick, sure sidearm throws to first.

Joe DiMaggio's powerful home-run swing is shown in this unusual classic photo taken at Yankee Stadium during batting practice.

Ike Caveney, manager of the San Francisco Seals, adjusts
the batting grip of his newest rookie, eighteen-year-old
Joe DiMaggio, in this exclusive photo taken in 1933.
DiMaggio played with the Seals for two seasons before his
contract was bought by the New York Yankees in 1935.

Joe DiMaggio hands his Army enlistment papers to Pfc.
J. H. Peck in an induction center in San Francisco and
volunteers for the Army during World War II. The date is
February 17, 1943. DiMaggio rose to the rank of sergeant
and served in the U. S. Army for 2½ years. A Navy yeoman
third class looks on, hoping that DiMag would go into the
Navy. But Joe became Private Joe DiMaggio within hours
after this photograph.

October 6, 1947: Yanks Defeat Dodgers to Win Series

The scene in the Yankee clubhouse was a riotous one on
October 6, 1947, for the Yankees had just defeated the
Brooklyn Dodgers to win the World Series. In the photo,
Yankee President Lee MacPhail is shown hugging Joe
DiMaggio and relief pitcher Joe Page, who starred through-
out the Series. Shortly after this photo was taken, Mac-
Phail resigned as Yankee president, selling his interest in
the club to Dan Topping and Del Webb.

The Yankees opened the 1948 season in Washington, D.C., by trimming the Senators, 12–4. Three of the stars of the game: Tommy Henrich (left) homered with a man on base; Allie Reynolds (right) also homered. Joe DiMaggio (center) homered and smacked out a three-base hit. In the back row is shortstop Phil Rizzuto.

DiMaggio Slams Two Homers Against Senators

Joe DiMaggio, the sensational Yankee slugger, trots home
to be congratulated by Yogi Berra (No. 8) after Joe drove
a home run out of the park in the first inning of a game
against the Washington Senators in July 1948. Two Yankees
were on base. This was the first game of a double-header.
DiMag slammed out another homer in the second game as
the Yanks took both games. Washington catcher Al Evans
looks on as umpire Ed Rommel signals the run in.

July 26, 1948

New York: Eluding several guards, this unidentified youngster managed to run onto the field at Yankee Stadium to
reach Joe DiMaggio in the outfield during the night game
of the Yankee-White Sox battle. He persuaded Joe, who
had hit two homers, to autograph his scrapbook.

Joe DiMaggio is shown sliding home after slashing a tremendous drive to deep center field at Yankee Stadium with two men on base. It was an inside-the-park homer for DiMag in a game against the Washington Senators on September 9, 1948. Catcher Al Evans of Washington straddles the plate vainly reaching for the ball as Joe crosses the plate. The Yanks won the ball game, 4–2.

He had to stop and throw overhand, giving the runner going down to first an extra couple of steps to beat the throw.

Fortunately for Joe, his fielding was forgotten each time he came to bat in the practice sessions. He battered the pitchers at the training camp mercilessly. None of them could get him out consistently. Joe just stood at the plate with his classic open stance and belted the ball to all corners of the ball park. In the dugout, Manager Caveney's eyes glowed as he watched Joe hit, and soon the local reporters at the camp began to ask questions about the sullen, quiet, poker-faced kid with the big bat.

One day Caveney called Joe over and told him Charley Graham wanted to see him. Caveney didn't keep Joe in suspense this time. "Graham wants you to sign a contract," he said.

DiMaggio rushed off the field to Graham's office. He didn't care what Graham was prepared to offer. He'd take anything, just to land with the Seals.

Graham, sitting benignly behind his desk, was waiting for Joe. He nodded DiMaggio to a seat and handed him a legal-looking document. "Read it, Joe," he said to the youngster.

DiMaggio skipped along, not understanding the legal language. He didn't care what it said, anyway. He just was itching to sign it. Suddenly he came across a paragraph he did understand. He read it through, unbelievingly. Then he read it again. He looked up at Graham.

"This says you're going to pay me two hundred and twenty-five dollars a month."

"That's right. Isn't that satisfactory?"

Joe gulped. Satisfactory! It was nearly double the

amount usually given to rookies with his lack of professional baseball background. He nodded. "I'll sign."

Graham smiled. He knew the figure was high. But Joe's hitting during the training-school sessions had convinced him that he had a "natural" on his hands. Joe DiMaggio was going to be one of the greatest hitters in the Pacific Coast League's history. This green kid, Graham felt, was worth the investment. As it turned out, Graham was right.

"You'll have to get your father down to sign the contract with you, Joe," Graham said. "You're not of legal age. You got to be twenty-one."

DiMaggio hesitated, embarrassed. "Pop doesn't know how to read or write English," he said, his face reddening.

"Anybody else in your family can come down and explain what it says to him?" Graham said. "You've got an older brother, haven't you?"

"I'll bring my brother Tom down," Joe said.

The next afternoon, while Papa DiMaggio sat listening, but not understanding a word, Tom explained about the contract. Papa DiMaggio shrugged. "If you say it's okay, Tomaso, it's okay for me, too," he said. "That is very good for Giuseppe. He's got a good job for a change—and two hundred and twenty-five dollars a month! That is very good. Let me make my name and go back to the boat."

Joe continued his spirited hitting when he reported to the Seals' regular training camp, and the reporters began to stalk him for feature stories. Joe, unsure of himself in the sudden limelight, inexperienced in talking to newspapermen, answered cryptically or, mumbling that he was busy, left the reporters standing with their pencils in midair. Small wonder then at the descriptions of DiMaggio as written in the San Francisco newspapers.

"A tall, gawky youngster, inclined to be rather surly for his age, is the talk of the Seals' training sessions," went one report. "He's Joe DiMaggio, brother of the Seals' outfielder Vince. He's tall, stringy, sullen, and tough to interview. The only talking this kid seems to do is with his bat. He's the best-looking hitter seen this spring. What he'll do when the regular season opens next week may be a different story, however. He is the most sullen player I've ever seen."

Now, some forty-five years later, the harsh, unfair criticism made of him during his first season with the Seals still bothers Joe. Numerous times, newspapermen have tried to explain DiMaggio's behavior during his early years with the Seals, and later with the Yankees. Nobody explains it so well and so simply as Joe himself.

"I was a kid—just eighteen years old—and I just didn't know how to act," he said. "As a kid I had never talked very much, and the guys I grew up with understood what kind of fellow I was. They knew I liked them even if I didn't know how to say it. I may have seemed dull and sullen to strangers, but I was just being natural. You know"—he smiled—"I remember the first time a San Francisco sportswriter asked me for a quote. I didn't know what a quote meant. I'm not ashamed to say it, I really didn't. I just looked at him. You can say I was pretty dumb, I guess. I looked at him, put my head down, scowled, and walked away."

For a while, when the Coast League season opened in April, it appeared that young Joe would get little chance to show anything. Opening day found him sitting on the Seals' bench, along with his brother Vince, who was then a second-term outfielder for the team.

Joe sat there, game after game, fretting at the inactivity. Aside from his eagerness to play, the thought kept running through his mind that a smart man like Charley Graham wouldn't keep paying someone two hundred and twenty-five dollars a month just to sit on the bench.

Several weeks after the season opened, Joe got his chance. Ed Stewart, also a rookie with the Séals, was playing right field. Though he had hit well during spring training, Stewart slumped badly and couldn't seem to get going. This day, midway through the game, Caveney called to Joe. "Hey, DiMaggio. Get in and pinch-hit for Stewart."

Joe heard the manager, but the meaning of what he said didn't penetrate for a moment. He continued sitting on the bench. "DiMaggio!" Caveney called sharply. "Get up there and hit, will ya! You're holding up the game!"

The startled youngster walked in a trance to the bat rack, picked out a club, and stepped into the batter's box. Fortunately, he was walked on four pitches. Joe was in such a state of excitement that to this day he does not remember how he reached first base.

The inning ended with Joe still on first. Automatically he trotted back into the dugout to regain his seat on the bench. But Caveney called to him again. "Joe, go out and play right field. Take it slow, you'll be all right."

Joe sat unmoving. Suddenly he felt an elbow jabbed sharply in his ribs. It was his brother Vince. "He means you, Joe. Didn't you hear him?"

Joe's jaw dropped. "Me? I never played the outfield in my life," he cried, almost in a panic.

"Yeah," Vince came back. "But you're playing it now. And you're getting paid for it, too."

Bewildered, DiMaggio picked up a glove and trotted out to right field. Thus, simply, was Joe DiMaggio con-

verted from a wild-armed infielder to a rifle-arme
outfielder, and a brilliant career begun.

Ike Caveney was a veteran and he had a way with
young players. He played DiMaggio in right field, along-
side an experienced center fielder, Joe Marty, who was
fast and strong, and with catcher Larry Woodall, Art
Garibaldi at second base, Vince DiMaggio a reserve
outfielder, and pitchers Ed Stutz, Jim Densmore, Bert
Cole, Winn Ballou, and Tom Sheehan, the Seals were
rated one of the strongest clubs in the Pacific Coast race.

Caveney sensed the blazing possibilities in Joe DiMaggio's big bat and was at his side constantly. Caveney was
attracted to the quiet, moody boy, realizing that Joe
needed and wanted help and someone to talk to. Caveney
was patient and understanding, and he worked long hours
with the young ballplayer.

After several errorless games in the field, Joe began to
feel comfortable and easy in the roomy green pastures of
the Seals' ball park. Base runners soon discovered that
DiMaggio had one of the most powerful arms they had
ever seen, and in short order, Joe's throwing feats were
the talk of the league. He still could not handle the
difficult line drives or pop flies hit to his field, but he covered an amazing amount of ground, and his strong arm
cut off many would-be runners at home plate.

But while his outfielding skills were improving, his hitting set the Coast League afire. On May 28 he started a
consecutive-game hitting streak that stretched to sixty-
one games before he was halted. It is still considered one
of the greatest feats of all time. During the course of the
amazing streak, which broke the previous league record
of forty-nine games, Joe brought new life and popularity
to baseball on the Pacific Coast.

9

The year 1933 was a terrible period of business Depression in the United States. The banks of the nation had to close their doors, millions of unemployed men and women walked the streets, and the bread lines of the hungry stretched endlessly. Money was scarce. Understandably, baseball games were certainly not included in people's tight budgets. Yet the poker-faced kid from Fisherman's Wharf practically saved the Pacific Coast League from bankruptcy. The big hitting streak started on May 28 before a handful of fans, and the day that Joe stretched his streak to fifty games, more than ten thousand frantic, howling baseball fans cheered him to the skies.

In the 1930s and 1940s the Coast League took its baseball seriously; but there was little attention paid to the DiMaggio streak until Joe had hit safely in twenty games. Most of the local sportswriters put it down to the first flash of a rookie hitter. "Just wait till the pitchers get a couple more looks at this kid," was the usual comment. "He'll be waving at the air just like everyone else."

When the streak got into the thirties, however, people

began to take notice. This looked like more than just rookie luck. And they began flocking to the parks to watch this sensational-hitting eighteen-year-old. Attendance picked up at every park the Seals visited for a series.

Most notable among Joe's new followers was Papa DiMaggio. With everyone talking about the sensational new player, he became interested in spite of himself. Unable to read English, Mr. DiMaggio had his family teach him the baseball symbols that appeared in the newspaper box score of each game so that he could follow his son's fortunes.

Each day during Joe's streak Papa would hurry home from the fishing boat, pick up a late-afternoon paper from a corner newsstand, and rush into the house to squint at the symbols on the sports page. "Hey, Mama, Giuseppe got two hits today. But he no hit a home run. What's the matter with that boy?"

Finally Mr. DiMaggio's curiosity got the best of him, and the family triumphantly bore him into the Seals' park to watch Joe play. The event was even more significant in view of the fact that Mr. DiMaggio had to miss his favorite afternoon diversion, his game of *bocci*. But he waved this aside with a good-humored grin.

"*Bocci?*" he exclaimed. "There's no money in *bocci!* Baseball, that's a smart game to play!"

DiMaggio's phenomenal hitting streak was not without its pressures. When his streak got to forty games, and he neared the all-time mark of forty-nine, it seemed even the pitchers were putting a little extra on every serve, wanting to be the man to stop the red-hot rookie.

Through it all, however, Joe seemingly remained unmoved. His bony features remained impassive. He neither frowned nor grinned at the plate or in the dugout. Only with the bat did he feel sure of himself. He still talked in monosyllables, if at all. He avoided reporters, embarrassed at their attention, and shied away from the ensuing publicity.

Naturally, a hitting streak like Joe's was full of narrow escapes. Several times his only hit of the game came in the ninth inning. Sometimes his hits were mere bloopers over the infield, or scratch infield singles. But, too, many a solid blast was hauled down in a great catch by an outfielder.

One of the really tight situations came up in the forty-third game. The Seals were playing Hollywood, who had Tom Sheehan, the former Yankee, on the mound that day. Sheehan was a crafty hurler; he had good stuff and could pitch to spots.

Going into the ninth inning the veteran hurler was riding a 12–1 margin over the Seals. He had baffled them all day, Joe DiMaggio included. Now Joe was at bat in the ninth, seven games away from Jack Ness's old mark of forty-nine games.

Sheehan, figuring that in his eagerness Joe would be swinging at anything, served his first two pitches wide of the plate. Suddenly Sheehan signaled for time and called his batterymate, Johnny Bassler, out to the mound for a conference.

"Say, Johnny," Sheehan said, "I was just thinking. If I walk this kid and bust his hitting streak, what do you think these San Francisco fans'll do to me?"

Bassler grinned sourly. "They'll probably hang you from the flagpole. Why don't you just lay it in there. We got 'em by eleven runs."

Sheehan scowled and thrust out his jaw. "Nothing doing. If this punk busher's going to get a hit off me, he's going to sweat for it like anybody else!"

The enraged hurler stamped around the mound, more than ever determined to get Joe out. He reared back and threw a blistering fast ball for a called strike. Joe fouled the next pitch for a two-and-two count.

Sheehan now figured he had the young rookie on the spot. DiMaggio wouldn't dare take the chance of getting a called strike three. He'd swing at anything. The big pitcher wound up and spun a snaky curve that broke off the outside of the plate. Joe leaned in as if to hit, then held back. It was ball three.

Sheehan then came back with his fast ball and Joe smacked it up the left-center-field alley in a line for a clean double. The Hollywood hurler called time and walked over to second base. He stuck out his hand to shake Joe's.

"I gotta hand it to you, kid. You had the guts to lay off that curve and wait for my fast one. You're gonna be a great batter."

The drama reached its highest pitch after Joe had hit in forty-eight straight games. If he hit in the next game, it would tie the record. The ninth inning of that forty-ninth game came up and Joe was hitless. And it looked as if he wouldn't even get a chance to bat. He was due to bat seventh. Four men had to reach base safely or the streak was over.

Joe's teammates made sure he got to bat. None of the men due up before him in the inning wanted to be in any way responsible for his failing to get the chance. Determinedly they slashed away at the opposing hurler. And

each of them got one base, though one man had to get hit
by a pitched ball to do it.

Up to the plate came DiMaggio, and the tension in the
ball park was unbearable. Hardly anyone even noticed
that the two runners waiting on the base paths represented the tying and winning runs of the ball game. Joe
was the only one who mattered.

The count went to two balls and two strikes. Then Joe
swung and fouled a pitch down the right-field line. Then
he took ball three. And he fouled another pitch. Finally
he lined a fast ball high off the left-field fence for a double. His forty-ninth straight game, tying the record! The
crowd went wild and hundreds of fans surrounded the
happy DiMaggio as he perched on second base.

In the Seals' locker room later, Joe's teammates were
kidding him about his streak. "Hey, Dead Pan," one
called to him, "get a good night's sleep tonight so you can
dream about breaking that record tomorrow."

Joe continued dressing silently. By now he was used to
his nickname—"Dead Pan." He was still stung occa-
sionally by some of his teammates' comments on his
aloofness, though he knew they meant well. Most of them
were older than he, and experienced. He felt like a new
kid on the block trying to break into the gang, and he
took the horseplay at his expense as part of the game.
Most of all he felt irritated and insecure as the sportswriters hounded him each day with questions, questions,
and more questions. And often not understanding some of
their talk, he simply remained silent. He didn't understand some of their big words and so he continued to remain quiet, aloof, and silent. And so he became "Dead
Pan" and "Poker-face" to them.

The next day more than ten thousand pop-eyed base-ball fans were out cheering the sensational freshman slugger to extend his amazing streak past the fifty mark, and when he singled in the very first inning of the game, hundreds of patrons, including Mayor Angelo Rossi of San Francisco, rushed onto the diamond to shake Joe's hand and wish him continued success.

The great crowds kept turning out up and down the West Coast as DiMaggio continued hitting. Finally after sixty-one games, Joe was stopped by pitcher Ed Walsh of the Oakland club. Joe had been raised to the lead-off spot in the batting order to give him more chances to bat, but though he hit the ball well in his five at-bats against Oakland, a fielder always managed to catch up with the ball.

Joe finished his first season with the Seals with a .340 batting average. He hit 28 home runs, led the league in runs batted in with 169, and, as evidence of his throwing skill, led the league in assists by an outfielder with 32.

His happiness was tempered, however, by the fact that his brother Vince was released by the Seals. Joe couldn't help but feel that his own success was partly responsible for Vince's outfield services being considered unnecessary to the team.

It was beginning to appear that Tom DiMaggio's prophecy about Joe and Vince was indeed an accurate one.

10

Luck never had much to do with the baseball career of Joe DiMaggio. Good luck, at least. After his first year with the Seals, the physical misfortune that was to plague Joe throughout his career began to dog him. Just to prove that this sensational rookie season was no fluke, Joe opened the 1934 campaign by slamming opposition pitchers all over the ball park. Into June he was still going strong. Then, after a double-header at Seal Park that month, an accident almost cut his career short right there.

Leaving the ball park, Joe hopped into a cab to visit one of his married sisters for dinner. Riding across town, his left foot fell asleep. When he got out of the cab, he stepped out first on his left foot and it crumpled under him. Joe toppled to the street hard.

He paid off the cab driver, and gritting his teeth against the terrible pain, hobbled to a nearby movie theater, the Milane, where he knew the manager. From there he was driven to the Emergency Hospital. As far as Joe was concerned, it was simply a sprain of some kind, and he was eager enough to accept the examining doctor's diagnosis that it was probably just that. He was told to go home and soak his knee in hot Epsom salts.

The following morning when Joe climbed out of bed, the leg buckled under him again. He began to worry. This early in his career, he didn't want to miss his turn in the Seals' lineup. Fortunately, there was no game scheduled for that day. Joe called Manager Ike Caveney and told him about the knee, but added he'd be ready to play the following day in Los Angeles.

Caveney, not taking any chances, kept Joe on the bench the next day. In the second game against Los Angeles, Joe was called on to pinch-hit. He walked stiffly up to the plate, covering his limp as best he could. He winced as he tried to dig his spikes into the dirt. Two called strikes shot past him as he struggled to regain his composure. Then he set himself and blasted the next pitch out of the park.

The fans seemed puzzled as Joe slowly limped around the bases instead of trotting. Manager Caveney was more suspicious than puzzled. When Joe came back to the bench the manager walked over to him. "How come that little stroll around the bases, Joe?" he said. "Your leg bothering you that bad?"

"No, no, Ike," Joe hastened to assure him. "I just figured I'd save the knee all I could, that's all. But I could have run if I wanted to."

Caveney nodded, but he wasn't satisfied. Two days later, when Joe pinch-hit again, the manager's fears were justified. Joe hit a long drive into left-center field that would have been a triple for even a slow runner. But Joe, hobbling and dragging his leg behind him, just managed to make second base. Caveney called for a pinch runner and sent Joe to the clubhouse.

Caveney followed close behind and ordered Joe to lie down on the rubbing table. Probing with his fingertips,

Caveney felt around the swollen knee area. Despite himself, Joe let out a pained gasp. Caveney looked up at him.

"What are you trying to do," he said to the young outfielder, "cripple yourself for good?"

DiMaggio swung his legs off the table. "It's only a bad sprain, Ike. In a couple of days I'll be okay again."

Caveney shook his head. "You're wrong, son. I'm shipping you back to San Francisco. You report to Dr. Bull when you get there and let him take a good look at that knee of yours. I'm calling him right now."

Dr. Bull, the club physician, took one look at Joe's swollen knee area and whistled. He probed gently with skilled fingers, at the same time watching Joe's face for expressions of pain. Finally he straightened up. "Well, son, I'll have to order X rays to be sure, of course. A trick knee can cause a lot of trouble. I think you've popped a few tendons in the knee joint."

"Is that serious, Doc?" Joe asked.

The physician smiled wryly. "Maybe not for an ordinary person. But I'll put it to you straight. You never know how it'll be with an athlete. It may pop out again any time after it's fixed. You're always taking a chance putting any extra strain on it. "But," he shrugged, "let's see what we can do to straighten you out now."

For three weeks Joe's left leg was packed ankle to thigh in an aluminum splint. And as he lay idle and fidgeting, anxious to get back into the lineup, reports came to him that the major-league scouts on his trail, originally eager to outbid each other for Joe's contract, had begun to sour on him. They were afraid to recommend purchase of a player with a knee that might pop out at any time and cripple him indefinitely.

Not all the scouts were so inclined, fortunately for

DiMaggio. Joe Devine and Bill Essick, two scouts for the New York Yankees, continued their interest in him. When he finally returned to the lineup, he managed to cover the outfield well enough and to continue his great hitting. But it was obvious that he was favoring his left leg. Then, a week later, Joe slipped on the dugout steps and the knee popped again. That was all for Joe DiMaggio for the 1934 season.

Aside from his injury, the season was a tremendous one for Joe. He had played in 101 games out of the possible 188 in the Pacific Coast League season, batting .341.

But there was still that black cloud that hung portentously over his future. As he sat gloomily at home with his leg once more heavily taped in splints, Joe couldn't help but wonder whether his playing days were over—or if a major-league team would ever take a chance on a "cripple," a fragile-limbed player who might never be good for anything but part-time duty.

The future looked very dim to Joe as the 1934 season neared its end. However, he hadn't counted on the bulldog tenacity of Bill Essick.

Yankee scout Bill Essick had watched DiMaggio closely, and saw that despite his accident, his speed was unimpaired, that he ran, not only as swiftly, but also as easily as before, that he pivoted smoothly at the plate. "Don't give up on DiMaggio," he phoned Ed Barrow, president of the Yankees. "Everybody out here in San Francisco thinks that I'm crazy. But I'm not. I think he's all right. Let me watch him for a couple of weeks more, and I'll have the final answer on him."

Barrow had great faith in Essick. "All right, Bill," he said. "Stick with him."

Two weeks later, Essick called Barrow again. "Ed, buy

DiMaggio," he said. "I think you can get him cheap. They're all laughing at me, but I know I'm right."

Barrow called Graham. "How much do you want for DiMaggio?" he asked.

"Forty thousand dollars."

"I'll give you twenty."

"Not a chance," Graham said.

They went on from there. Graham knew that no other major-league club was willing to take a chance on Joe. He also knew that Barrow knew it. He put up a battle as long as he could for forty thousand dollars, but finally settled for twenty-five thousand dollars. It was the greatest buy in the history of modern baseball. "But before we actually sign a contract for the deal," said Barrow, "here's what I propose.

"We'd like you to send DiMaggio to Dr. Spencer in Los Angeles for an examination. He's a top man with bone injuries and he's helped a lot of players. If the doc says DiMaggio's leg will be okay, the Yankees will wrap up a deal for him."

"What's the entire deal?" Graham asked.

"Assuming Dr. Spencer says DiMaggio will be okay, the Yankees will go for a sum of money not to exceed twenty-five thousand dollars in cash; we'll also send the Seals two pitchers, two infielders, and an outfielder. We figure that adds up to about a total of seventy-five thousand dollars for the DiMaggio contract. That's a whale of a lot of money," said Barrow. "We intend farming out DiMaggio to our team in Newark. If he looks okay there he goes up with the Yanks."

Graham picked up the phone and dialed Joe's number

at home. "How soon do you want to have him report up to Los Angeles?" he asked the Yankee scout.

Essick grinned. "Tell DiMaggio to start packing his bags."

The New York Yankees either had utmost faith in the healing powers of Dr. Spencer—or confidence in Joe DiMaggio's capacity to rebound physically—for early in November, even before Dr. Spencer started to treat Joe's leg, the club announced they had bought an option on DiMaggio's services.

According to the terms of the deal, Joe was to play the complete 1935 season with the Seals, then report to the Yankees the following spring if they picked up their option.

Although DiMaggio may have been shy in public and rather backward when being interviewed by newspapermen, he was, with his brother Tom's urging, far from shy at contract-signing time. In 1934 Joe was paid four hundred and fifty dollars a month by the Seals for a six-month season, a total of twenty-seven hundred dollars. Without being boastful, he knew he was worth more to the Seals both as a player and as an attraction at the gate.

The Seals offered him a substantial increase that would bring him close to five thousand dollars for the 1934 campaign. Joe wanted more. Together with his brother Tom he demanded sixty-five hundred dollars plus 15 per cent of the twenty-five thousand dollars the Seals would get from the Yankees when and if the New York club picked up their option on him.

The Seals balked at the deal. Joe refused to sign the

contract. Into early March of 1935 the battle went on. Joe threatened to quit baseball entirely if the Seals refused to meet his demands.

"My brother Tom owns a boat—and together we can make money catching and selling crabs," Joe announced truculently. "I'm not signing with the Seals unless I'm satisfied."

Joe's old friends, of course, remembering well his aversion to fishing—and especially crab fishing—put little stock in Joe's threat. And Charley Graham, the Seals' president, put the talk down to the youthful sulkiness of his twenty-year-old slugger. But Graham didn't delude himself about the seriousness of Joe's holdout, and he knew he'd have to give in, sooner or later.

The most puzzled man of all throughout the contract negotiations was the new manager of the Seals, Lefty O'Doul. A great batting star during his years with the Phillies, the Dodgers, and the Giants, O'Doul had been hired as a playing manager to replace Ike Caveney. Lefty, a colorful, garrulous man who lived and loved baseball, couldn't understand DiMaggio's attitude at all.

"I don't know much about this fishing business," he commented, "though I was born here in San Francisco myself. But even suppose DiMaggio could make good money at it, look at the hours he'd have to work to get it."

O'Doul was half kidding, but long before he was to see DiMaggio at the Seals' training camp, Joe was visited by an old friend of his who was all seriousness. It was Ike Caveney, his former manager. Joe was more upset than surprised at seeing Caveney.

"What brings you down here, Ike?" he asked. "Graham send you to get me to sign?"

Caveney ignored the question. "Hello, Joe, how've you been? Whatsa matter, aren't you glad to see me?"

"Yeah, sure, Ike, it's always nice to see you," Joe said. Actually, he had lots of respect for Caveney, remembering how Ike had taken him under his wing and improved his hitting and fielding. Caveney had spotted his potential as an outfielder when he was floundering at shortstop. But he still had the feeling that Caveney was sent over by the Seals' management to work on him.

"You know you're always welcome here," Joe said to Caveney. "But if you came to talk about my signing—"

Caveney held up his hand. "You're still running the bases with your head down, I see, Joe. Let's the two of us get something straight right from the start. I'm not stooging for Graham or anybody else. Nobody even knows I'm down here to see you. I came on my own, because—well, because I think you got a great future at stake in baseball and I want to make sure you know what you're doing."

Joe sat silent a long moment. "I got to get more money," he said flatly.

Caveney threw up his hands, exasperated. "Is that all you got to say?" he demanded.

Joe shrugged. "My brother Tom handles my business. That's all I can tell you, Ike."

The following week, when Joe left for Los Angeles with scout Bill Essick to see Dr. Spencer, Joe indicated that he would report to the Seals' spring training camp at Fresno when his knee had mended. Two weeks later, Joe showed up at camp, in uniform but still unsigned. That afternoon, however, Graham phoned the camp from San Francisco, where he had gone to confer with Tom Di-

Maggio. The new contract offer had been accepted. He would return to Fresno immediately to have Joe sign.

Joe, meanwhile, was chasing fungos in the outfield, testing his knee. He had the batting coach hit the ball to his left and to his right, pop the ball short into the outfield, then hit one over his head, trying out the effects of the various pressures.

Along a foul line, watching intently, stood the Seals' bespectacled trainer, Bobby Johnson. "Look at him go," Johnson said admiringly. "He moves just like a deer. It's good to see him back here. He's a fine ballplayer and he's going to be one of the greatest soon."

Joe's stoutest boosters rubbed their eyes when the Seals met the Chicago Cubs in an exhibition game. On the mound for Chicago was Lon Warneke, who had won twenty-two games the year before and was to go on to win twenty during the coming season.

All Joe did was go three-for-three against Warneke, including a double and a triple, and when the Cubs' other ace, Larry French, came on to finish, Joe greeted him with a line single through the box that had the veteran hurler leaping for his life.

O'Doul, the Seals' new manager, took to the young outfielder from the first. He recognized a great player in the making, and though Joe was a "natural" hitter, O'Doul, no mean slugger in his own right, ironed out the rough spots in Joe's batting style.

The knee was apparently restored to normal by Dr. Spencer's treatments, but Joe took things easy, working, exercising the knee, taking the whirlpool treatments, and running in the outfield. He missed a good part of spring training and got away slowly when the regular season started. But in May Joe began to hit, and as the Seals' pitching folded, only Joe's bat kept the team in the winning columns.

A perfect day at the plate was not unusual when Joe started on his hot streak. Two hits a day, three hits a day became the expected. While his hitting fell off slightly in June, he continued to slug consistently for the rest of the 1935 season.

When the final tabulations were in, Joe had hit .398 for the year, finishing less than a percentage point, actually, behind the league-batting champ, Ox Eckhardt. Joe's percentage was .398, Eckhardt's .399.

Most of Joe's hits, too, were for extra bases, a true indication of the power of his slugging. He rapped 34 home runs, 58 doubles, and 18 triples, a total of 110 extra-base hits out of the 173 he got that season. And he batted across the plate 154 runs.

The Yankees surprised no one by picking up their option on Joe at the close of the 1935 baseball campaign. At twenty-five thousand dollars and five players, it was considered the buy of the century.

11

The exciting prospect of playing with the New York Yankees didn't dim Joe DiMaggio's business sense. He returned the first contract the New York club sent him, which would have paid him eight hundred and twelve dollars a month. Joe wanted one thousand, two hundred and fifty dollars a month. The Yankees sent him a second contract, with a slight increase. Joe sent that one back, too. The salary hassle continued through January and into February before DiMaggio and the Yankees got together at somewhere around one thousand, one hundred dollars a month.

Joe's parents saw him off to the Yankees' spring-training camp rather sadly. Though of course proud and happy for him, this would be the first time Joe was leaving the West Coast area. Eight months of the year, they knew, they would only be reading about their Giuseppe.

However, they sent him off in good hands. Two Yankee infielders were escorting Joe to Florida—Tony Lazzeri and Frankie Crosetti. Both men were from San Francisco, and Lazzeri kind of adopted DiMaggio as his charge, just as he had Crosetti a few years before.

Actually, you couldn't have found three more perfectly

suited traveling companions anywhere. They were probably the three most taciturn men in baseball, and it is quite likely that not more than a few minutes of conversation passed among them during the entire trip to St. Petersburg, and it was the older more experienced Tony Lazzeri who spoke.

Lazzeri did manage to give Joe lots of advice.

"Now listen, Joe," he said to his new ward, "I want to straighten you out on how to act when you get down South with the club. And I'm not pulling any punches, see? You're one of us, like Frankie here and me, you understand, Joe? Just a punk kid from the lots of 'Little Italy.' Maybe you were a big shot with the Seals, but you're just another kid trying to take somebody's job now. Am I right, Frankie?" he said to Crosetti.

The Yankee shortstop nodded.

"You're gonna get the needle plenty when you get down to Florida, Joe. You're gonna get it from the sportswriters. You come down with a big reputation, and they're all gonna be out for blood. Right, Frankie?"

Crosetti simply nodded again.

"There's only one thing you gotta do, Joe. And if you don't learn this you're gonna be miserable—in hot water from the start. You gotta learn to keep your mouth shut. Tight. Somebody asks you a question, try to say yes or no or you don't know and forget about it. Don't start talking about how you're gonna hit or gonna field or what you did with the Seals. That's the worst thing you can do, pop off about how good you are. You got me straight, Joe?"

"I sure have, Tony," DiMaggio answered. "But don't worry about me. I don't like to talk much anyway, especially to guys I don't know."

"Good boy," Lazzeri said. "Remember, just keep your mouth shut and you're gonna be all right."

Naturally quiet as he was, however, DiMaggio found the advice a little hard to follow when he pulled into the Yankees' camp. When Lazzeri took him into the clubhouse at Miller Huggins Field and started introducing him around, the war was on.

Most of the players merely nodded at the introduction, but Red Ruffing, the great pitcher, looked Joe up and down and drawled with mock awe. "So you're the great DiMaggio. I hear you hit .400 on the Coast. Well, kid, you ought to hit .800 here, because we play with a shiny new ball and every time you nick one they'll throw in a brand-new, shiny one."

Joe reddened and Lazzeri glared at Ruffing, but the big hurler chuckled and turned back to his locker.

Lefty Gomez was even rougher on young DiMaggio. "So you're the guy that did his brother out of a job," he said when he met Joe.

DiMaggio looked at Gomez questioningly. "What do you mean?"

"Wasn't your brother Vince playing with Frisco when you came to them?" Gomez asked.

"Yes," Joe admitted.

"And didn't he help you get on the Seals in the first place?"

"Sure he did."

"And after you got on, didn't the Seals let Vince go?"

"Yes, but—"

"So that's just what I said, you did your brother out of his job."

"Yes, but—" Joe tried to explain, but Gomez broke into

a loud guffaw. It was weeks later that Joe learned that Gomez, a great practical joker and clubhouse kidder, was merely joking. As a matter of fact, Gomez became one of the few close friends DiMaggio ever had in baseball. In the meantime, however, Joe was feeling pretty miserable after his first round of introductions to his new team-mates.

Only Lou Gehrig, that first day, made DiMaggio feel welcome. He shook Joe's hand with his huge one, and smiled his greeting. "Nice to have you with us, Joe," the big first baseman said.

Following Lazzeri's advice, Joe swallowed his hurt, and when the spring series of exhibition games began, he let his bat and his arm do the talking for him. His first time up in a Yankee uniform, he faced Bill Walker, the veteran Cardinal southpaw, and on the second pitch boomed a tremendous triple over the center fielder's head. He got two more hits that game, and went on through the first five games hitting at a .625 clip.

Then his bad luck returned to plague him.

Playing against the Boston Braves, Joe slid into third, legging out a triple. As he slammed into the bag he upset Joe Coscarart, the third baseman, who fell heavily onto Joe's left foot. It didn't seem like much of a bump, but it was painful, and Joe left the game to give the trainer a good look at the damage.

Earle Painter, the Yankees' trainer, took a look at the swelling around Joe's ankle and prescribed rest.

"Just a couple of days off it, Joe, and you'll be okay," Painter said. "And take a little baking under the diathermy lamp, too; that'll help."

Diathermy lamps, however, can be tricky, and Joe was

not accustomed to using one. He stayed under the lamp too long the second day, and came up with a badly burned foot. The Yankees called in a doctor to look at the burn. The news was bad. "This man will not be able to play for two or three weeks," the doctor said.

So the debut of Joe DiMaggio as a New York Yankee was to be delayed. And since the Yankees were due to leave St. Petersburg and start North on an exhibition tour that would take them to Washington on Opening Day, Manager Joe McCarthy decided to ship DiMaggio on ahead.

"No sense in having you trail along on that bum foot," the manager said to Joe. "You go on to New York. Maybe you can break in during the home series there."

DiMaggio nodded glumly. From the first day he'd met McCarthy, Joe had decided the Yankee manager was a great man. McCarthy hadn't made a fuss over Joe, nor had he ignored him, either. But he had a quiet way of making DiMaggio feel that he had confidence in him.

Joseph Vincent McCarthy had never played a game of ball in the major leagues. He was born in Philadelphia, April 21, 1887, attended grade schools and high school there, played sandlot ball, and went to Niagara University at Buffalo for a while. Then he quit his books to join the Wilmington club of the Tri-State League in 1906. Square-jawed, tenacious, he made the most of his limited ability as a ball player by the thoroughness with which he studied the game and the zeal with which he played it. A year and a half with Wilmington, a half year with Franklin in the Inter-State League, and he made the jump to Toledo in the American Association.

He spent 3½ years at Toledo, playing the infield. In 1911 he was sold to Indianapolis. He was appointed

manager of the Wilkes-Barre team in 1913. From there
Joe went to Louisville, where he played second base and
made quite a reputation as one of the best infielders in
the minor leagues.

In 1919 he was appointed manager of the Louisville
team and within two years he won his first pennant. And
soon the baseball men around the country began to talk
about him. They said he was one of the very best, perhaps
the best minor-league manager. When he again won the
pennant in 1925, he was hired by William Wrigley, owner
of the Chicago Cubs, to manage the team. And under
McCarthy, the Cubs finished fourth in 1927, third in
1928. By 1930, with the addition of the great Rogers
Hornsby, the Chicago Cubs won the pennant, but lost the
World Series to the Athletics.

The Yankees were very good in 1931, McCarthy's first
year, as manager, but the Philadelphia Athletics again
beat them out for the pennant as the Bronx Bombers with
Babe Ruth, Lou Gehrig, Tony Lazzeri, Earl Combs, Bill
Dickey, Lefty Gomez, Red Ruffing, George Pipgras, Ben
Chapman, and the crafty curve-ball star, Herb Pennock,
finished a close second. But in 1932 the promise of a
championship was fulfilled as McCarthy piloted his Yankees to a pennant, and then went on to defeat his old
team, the Chicago Cubs, to win the World Series.

McCarthy had hit the very top of baseball in a sus-
tained drive that carried across two seasons. Now, as 1933
came on, the momentum slowed, and he was to know
three years of bitter disappointment before he would win
another championship.

That was in 1936, the year Joe DiMaggio joined the
club.

A strict disciplinarian, with a triggerlike baseball mind,

McCarthy had his hands full handling the tempestuous Babe Ruth through five stormy years, but McCarthy and his firm hand won out even over the greatest slugger in baseball history. Joe had handled hundreds of young ballplayers and older ones too and he knew at first meeting Joe DiMaggio that Joe would be handled best by leaving him alone. There was a certain spark—an immediate understanding between the young San Francisco ballplayer and McCarthy, and after watching but one afternoon of practice McCarthy knew that DiMaggio had the stamp of greatness. All he had to do was to guide and mold the quiet young man from San Francisco.

When McCarthy announced to the sportswriters that DiMaggio would be his left fielder that season, it gave the youngster quite a boost. It was no longer a question of winning a job to Joe. Now he felt he had to make good to justify the confidence McCarthy had in him.

McCarthy, for his part, had more hope than confidence. He had led the Yankees to a world championship in 1932, then three years in a row finished second. Coming so close but not quite winning was a constant worry. If he didn't win this year his job was on the line. DiMaggio, he prayed, might make the difference between getting beat out again and coming out on top. He could field and he could hit.

On paper, the Yankees did look as if they might beat the Detroit Tigers this year. The Tigers, under Mickey Cochrane, were the world champions after beating the Cubs in the 1935 World Series, and the Tigers had two pennants in a row under their belts.

Besides DiMaggio, who was put in left field by McCarthy, the Yankees had hard-hitting—but unpredictable—Ben Chapman in center and George Selkirk in right field. Lou Gehrig, of course, was on first, Tony Lazzeri on second, Frank Crosetti at short, and Red Rolfe at third. Behind the plate was Bill Dickey, directing a formidable battery that included Red Ruffing, Lefty Gomez, Monte Pearson, Bump Hadley, and veteran relief pitcher Johnny Murphy, heading the bullpen brigade.

Despite the lineup, the Yankees lost the opening game at the Stadium against the Boston Red Sox. As Joe dismally sat watching from the bench, the Yankees fanned the air vainly against Sox hurler Lefty Grove. And in the field they bobbled the ball and missed throws. Red Ruffing lost the decision, and the papers the next day predicted another pennant for the Tigers. The general consensus was that the Yankees showed nothing more than they had the year before.

It wasn't until May 3 that the Yankees finally exhibited the secret weapon they lacked the year before. Manager McCarthy shrewdly kept Joe out of the lineup a few extra days to make sure the foot was completely healed. The pressure on the rookie, he knew, would be tremendous. The fans in the grandstand had been chanting for days now, "We want DiMaggio." The press was waiting to see what he would do in a real major-league game. His teammates were waiting. And McCarthy, too, was waiting.

Would Joe DiMaggio turn out to be a bust, another minor-league sensation who flopped in the big leagues—another "spring violet" who bloomed in spring exhibition games but wilted under the pressure of playing for keeps?

On May 3, 1936, Joe DiMaggio boomed out his answer.

12

Jack Knott, the pitcher for the St. Louis Browns, looked up at the overcast sky, then down at the batter digging in at the plate. This rookie Joe DiMaggio isn't what he's cracked up to be, he thought. Got him in the first inning on a slow curve. An easy grounder to the third baseman. He's too eager. That slow stuff will get him. He's too tense.

Knott hitched at his belt and took the sign from his batterymate. Knott coiled and spun a slow curve that missed the corner for a ball. A fast ball over the inside was good for a strike. Then he came back with the slow curve, this time inside. DiMaggio's bat flashed and cracked the pitch on a line into left field for a single. His first major-league hit! And the big crowd at Yankee Stadium, attracted by the Yankees' announcement that DiMaggio would play, roared as he pulled into first base.

The Yankees seemed to come alive now, and they belted the Browns' pitcher to the showers. In the sixth inning, Joe came up again and blasted a tremendous triple off Elon Hogsett to the flagpole in center field. The crowd went wild; even the normally imperturbable McCarthy grinned.

Joe wasn't through yet. In the ninth he singled again, for his third hit of the day, as the Yankees won the game, 14–5.

With DiMaggio in the lineup the Yankees began to move. The rookie from the Coast hit safely in sixteen straight games. In three weeks the Yankees moved from the second division to first place, and there seemed little doubt that as long as Joe remained healthy, the pennant would fly over Yankee Stadium come October.

Gratified as Manager McCarthy was with Joe's spectacular hitting, it was the outfielder's defensive maneuvers that really warmed McCarthy's heart; for Joe was playing one of the toughest outfields in the business, Yankee Stadium's "sun field," so called because the sun shone directly onto the left-field section all during a day game, forcing a fielder to follow fly balls through a blinding glare.

But Joe grabbed everything hit his way, loping with that smooth, graceful stride that was beginning to become his trademark. And in his first week in the lineup he showed overeager base runners that he had developed one of the most accurate throwing arms in baseball.

In the second game of a Sunday double-header with Detroit, the Yankees were holding a 6–5 lead in the ninth inning. There was one out, men on first and third for Detroit. Charley Gehringer then hit a long fly ball to left field, and as DiMaggio set himself under the hit, Pete Fox, representing the tying run, tagged up at third.

Joe hauled in the fly ball, and Fox took off for home. DiMaggio cut loose a fantastic throw to catcher Dickey that boomed in on the fly right across home plate, and Fox was tagged out to end the game.

The crowd went hysterical. It was one of the greatest

throws ever seen anywhere, and as DiMaggio trotted in to the dugout he was given a hero's shower of torn paper and shredded scorecards from the grandstand seats.

His popularity with the fans was growing each day, and when the Yankees returned from their first western trip, a police escort had to help Joe get into Yankee Stadium. The crowd cheered him on every appearance on the field. Out in the center-field bleacher section one day, an Italian flag was draped over the railing by a newly formed DiMaggio fan club.

"On that first road trip," said Jimmy Ceres, a sports buff and constant companion, "DiMaggio was very quiet, but friendly. There were some who insisted that he was inaccessible then and suspicious of every writer. I found him easy to be with, and his constant pals were Lefty Gomez and Pat Malone, both pitchers with the team. We had a lot of laughs that first season. Gomez wasn't called Goofy for nothing. There was a banquet for Joe in every town he played. Old men of Italian descent who never saw a ball game before turned out in great numbers. They liked to sit in the bleachers because they were nearest to Joe.

"There was the time in Detroit," Ceres continued, "when DiMaggio asked me if I liked Italian food, and I said I did."

"Meet me in the lobby after the game," said Joe. "They're giving a dinner for me in a spaghetti joint. It's great food."

"I came down to the lobby," said Jimmy, "and asked one of the Yankees where Joe was. They told me he was in the dining room. He was eating a full-course dinner . . . steak, mixed green salad, and french-fried potatoes.

"If the Italian food is so great," said Ceres, "why are you ducking it?"

"I'm not," said Joe, "I'm just having a little snack."

"Later," said Ceres, "we went to the Italian dinner and Joe dug in and ate everything served to him."

When gifts began pouring in and dinner parties were thrown in honor of Joe, Yankee boss Ed Barrow started worrying about the size of DiMaggio's head. He called Joe into his office one day.

"DiMaggio," he said, "you're doing great, and the fans all love you. I'm glad to see it, glad to see you make good —for yourself and for the Yankees. But a word of good advice. Don't take all the cheers too seriously. And don't start pressing to keep up the pace and your popularity. Just play your game and let everything else take its course."

"You don't have to worry about me, Mr. Barrow," Joe said. "I don't get excited easy."

If Joe had entertained any thoughts about being a superman, they were cut short by the All-Star game in July. The American League had won the first three games of the annual classic started in 1933. Now the American Leaguers saw little reason why they should not repeat, especially with Joe DiMaggio in the lineup. Joe had been given quite an honor by being picked for the squad, since he was only a rookie. But all eyes were on him that day in Braves Field, expecting all kinds of miracles.

What they got, of course, was summed up in the headlines next day:

DIMAGGIO GOAT OF FIRST ALL-STAR
AL DEFEAT

His first time up in the first inning, with a man on first, Joe rapped into a double play against Dizzy Dean. In the second inning Joe charged a low line drive by Gabby Hartnett, and trying for a shoestring catch, let the ball get by him for a triple.

In the fourth inning Joe popped to Leo Durocher at shortstop. In the fifth Joe juggled a single by Billy Herman, and Billy took second on the error. Herman then scored on Joe Medwick's single with what turned out to be the winning run.

Joe got a few more chances to redeem himself at the plate, but failed miserably. In the sixth he dribbled back to pitcher Carl Hubbell. In the seventh, with the bases loaded and two out, he bounced easily to Leo Durocher.

Joe got his last chance in the ninth. His team was one run behind. Charley Gehringer was on second with the tying run. Two were out. Joe cut at the first pitch and popped weakly to Herman at second and the game was over.

The All-Star game proved that Joe DiMaggio was not yet a superstar. But more important, and to Joe's advantage, it showed he could not be shaken by adversity—for right after the midsummer event he continued assaulting the pitchers and fielding in flawless style.

Joe's feats made good copy for the sportswriters, who began comparing him with baseball immortals like Babe Ruth, Bob Meusel, and Tris Speaker. There was a resemblance to Speaker and Meusel in Joe's fielding style, but in hitting, unlike Ruth, Joe was a late swinger with great control over the bat.

The awesome quality about the Bambino was his raw power. Ruth swung at everything from the heels, often committing himself to a swing before he recognized the type of pitch coming in. This accounted for his great number of strike-outs. DiMaggio, with his powerful arms and keen eye, waited until the last moment, then flashed his bat around with a great wrist motion. This not only cut down on his strike-outs, but also made Joe a batter without an apparent weakness.

Opposing hurlers tried everything, but couldn't find a consistent pitch that would get Joe out. They threw him high and low, inside and out, fast and slow curves, everything in the book. They might get him with a pitch one time, only to have him slam the same serve out of the park the next time.

His fielding combined the best of Meusel and Speaker. Like Tris, Joe had tremendous range afield, and in June of his freshman year McCarthy took advantage of this to switch Joe into center field, and, like Meusel, Joe set himself for the throw as he was making the catch. A single to center field usually sends a runner from first to third—but not, however, when a ball was hit out DiMaggio's way.

By August the American League pennant race was over except for the statistics. The Yankees had opened up a lead of ten games and battered the rest of the league into submission. Bitterly, Manager Joe Cronin of the Red Sox fingered the cause of the Yankees' runaway.

"It's that DiMaggio," he complained to the sportswriters. "He's upset the whole balance of the league. The Yankees got about the same team this year that they had last year when they came in second. Except for DiMaggio. He's hot and he got the whole team hot. He stays that way and they'll be the team to beat for the next ten years," Cronin predicted.

On September 9 the Yankees clinched the pennant, setting an American League record. No club had ever won as early as that before. They finished the season 19½ games in front of the second-place Tigers.

DiMaggio had a few notations set down next to his name, too, after his rookie season. His outstanding performances included 206 hits for a rookie, tying a major-league record by hitting 2 home runs in an inning (on June 24), leading the league in triples with 15 and in assists by an outfielder with 22.

His season's average was .323, including, besides the 15 triples, 44 doubles and 29 home runs. He batted in 125 runs and had a fielding average of .978.

It was a tremendous showing for a rookie, or any player. Had Joe not been a rookie, however, the performance would have attracted little attention that year, for the 1936 Yankees were one of the greatest slugging teams in history.

Bill Dickey led the team in hitting with a .362 average, Gehrig hit .354, DiMaggio .323, Rolfe .319, Selkirk .308, Jake Powell .299, Crosetti .288, and Lazzeri .287.

Gehrig also hit 49 home runs, DiMaggio 29, Dickey 22, Selkirk 18, Crosetti 15, Lazzeri 14, Rolfe 10, and Powell 8.

It was this punch that won the pennant. The Yankees had only one 20-game winner, Red Ruffing, who won just 20. The great relief artist Johnny Murphy, however, won 12 and saved as many more.

All in all, the Yankees looked like a good bet to win the World Series. For the first time since 1923 New York was to have a "subway series." Bill Terry's Giants were to face the Yankees, and the war drums began beating in the Bronx.

13

It was a miserable day for a ball game. Rain fell intermittently and a cold wind blew in from the river, but a capacity crowd packed the Polo Grounds to see Red Ruffing face the Giant ace, Carl Hubbell, who had won twenty-six games that year. And the Giant fans came to see the much-heralded rookie, Joe DiMaggio.

The great Hubbell, of course, was no respecter of records. The Yankee bombers were just another ball club to him, and he started the Giants off on the winning foot by beating the American League rivals, 6–1. The game was a lot closer than the score indicated, however.

As the Yankees came to bat in the eighth, they trailed only 2–1. With one out, Crosetti was on third and Rolfe on first as the result of a double and a bunt single. And up to the plate strode DiMaggio. Joe had reached Hubbell for a single earlier in the game. Now, on a two-two pitch, Joe hit a low line drive that appeared headed for right-center field. But second baseman Burgess Whitehead lunged desperately at the ball and caught it, and still on his knees doubled Rolfe off first to end the inning.

For the records, all Joe did was smack into a rally-killing double play. A foot more to the right and he could have been a hero. As it was, the Giants scored four more times in their half of the eighth to wrap up the first game of the Series.

It rained the second day, too, and the game was held over. Maybe that day off did the trick for the Yankees, for they put on a hitting exhibition yet to be equaled in a World Series. All sorts of history was made, not the least of which were the presence in the stands of President Franklin D. Roosevelt, Joe's mother, and his brother Tom.

The bombardment began in the first inning, as the Yankees scored twice. But in the third they leveled in earnest on Hal Schumacher and sent the Giants' No. 2 hurler scurrying to the showers with a seven-run outburst. Four more Giant pitchers were thrown into the fray, but the slaughter continued. The Yankees closed out the game by ramming home six more runs off Harry Gumbert. Final score: Yankees 18, Giants 4.

Twelve records were tied or broken in this game. DiMaggio accounted for one tied mark by making three put-outs in one inning, the ninth. And on two of them he stole base hits away from the batter.

Lefty Gomez, the Yankee pitcher in this game, was just getting the ball across the plate by the time the Giants came to bat in the ninth. Joe Moore opened the Giants' half with a soft fly to DiMaggio. Dick Bartell doubled. Bill Terry then smacked a sinking line drive to left-center that was headed for extra bases. But Joe swooped in and made a great catch right off the top of the grass to retire the Giants' manager.

For the third out Joe was sent in the opposite direction. Hank Lieber, the big center fielder, smacked a fast ball

high over DiMaggio's head in straightaway center. Joe
was off at the crack of the bat. He turned his back on
home plate and scurried to deep center field. He went almost as far as he could go, near the clubhouse steps in
right-center, turned his head at the last minute, and
caught the ball on the dead run. The magnificent catch
ended the ball game.

Joe wasn't lacking in the hitting department, either, for
this game. He rapped a double and two singles, scored
twice, and batted in two runs.

In the third game, played at Yankee Stadium, Bump
Hadley of the Yankees squeezed out a 2–1 win over Fred-
die Fitzsimmons. The Giants' pitcher gave up only four
hits, one a double by DiMaggio, but the Yankees got
them when they counted, and one was a homer by Lou
Gehrig.

Monte Pearson beat Hubbell in the fourth game, 4–2,
and the Yankees needed just one more to win the Series.
But Hal Schumacher pitched a great clutch game to win
for the Giants in the tenth inning, 5–4. In trouble most of
the way, Schumacher left nine men stranded on the bases.
He fanned ten Yankees, including DiMaggio twice. In the
third inning, with the bases loaded and nobody out, he
got DiMaggio and Gehrig on successive strike-outs, and
got Bill Dickey to pop out.

The Yankees went into the ninth inning of the sixth
World Series game holding a slim 6–5 lead. They wanted
this game badly, for if the Giants tied the Series then,
they'd have Carl Hubbell back on the mound the next
day.

DiMaggio opened the ninth with a sharp single to left.
Gehrig followed with a single, and DiMaggio sped to

third. In the third-base coaching box Art Fletcher danced up and down jubilantly. "Come on, Joe, get this one across and we're in." Joe knew full well the importance of his run. A team two runs behind has to play the game differently from a one-run-behind situation.

Bill Dickey was up now. He took a ball, then a strike. He cut at the next pitch and tapped a slow roller down the first-base line. DiMaggio charged toward the plate, Bill Terry charged down off first at the ball.

As Terry came up with the ball, DiMaggio stopped halfway down the line, watching to see what Terry would do. If he threw to the catcher, Hank Danning, he'd have to try to get back to third. If Terry charged across the diamond right at Joe, DiMaggio was in trouble; he'd have to break one way or the other, and Terry could then throw him out.

He watched Terry carefully. The Giants' first baseman cocked his arm and threw; but toward third base. DiMaggio flew toward the plate. Eddie Mayo, the third baseman, threw to the catcher. Danning got the throw in time and crouched, blocking the plate. But DiMaggio barreled in and dove headfirst around Danning, sweeping his hand over home plate as he slid by. In the cloud of dust that enveloped the scene the crowd could still make out the flat palms of the umpire gesturing "Safe!"

A great roar went up from the stands. The Yankees, on the offensive now, pushed through the hole opened up by DiMaggio. They scored six more times in that frame, winning the game, 13–5, and the World Series, 4 games to 2.

This, his first World Series, was DiMaggio's best hitting series. He batted .346 and knocked in 3 runs. He never surpassed either the batting average or the 9 hits he gathered for the Series.

It was, as a matter of fact, a magnificent all-round year for DiMaggio and even greater because it was the year he was on trial in a Yankee uniform. There was no doubt by now that he belonged in it as much as any of the great Yankee veterans.

DiMaggio took the train back to San Francisco a happy young man of twenty-one. Only one thing bothered him: He hadn't hit it off too well with some of the New York baseball writers. It was, he admitted, largely his own fault.

"I just don't know why," Joe told a friend before he left for San Francisco, "but I couldn't seem to get friendly with them. Every time they'd want to talk to me, I'd kind of freeze up. I guess I was just nervous, as usual. But it's one thing I sure do regret about this year. I guess some of them think I'm swellheaded or something. But it isn't so. They're a bunch of nice guys, most of them, and I hope we get along better next year."

The fact was that some of the writers did put Joe down as a surly, swellheaded rookie who was making himself deliberately tough to talk to. Despite the fact that Joe had come to New York with a reputation for taciturnity, some New York writers took an immediate dislike to Joe's seeming coldness. This was to remain a sore spot between Joe and some sections of the press for the remainder of his career. But Joe pulled into his hometown well content with things. He was the conquering hero in his old neighborhood. He had his own apartment in fashionable North Beach, but whenever he could get away from the luncheons and banquets in his honor, or the sports events at which he was asked to officiate, he wandered back to Taylor Street and Fisherman's Wharf, looking for old friends.

On bright afternoons he camped himself in a chair on the sunny side of a filling station run by Vito Vattaglia, one of his sandlot friends. The two friends, sitting and dozing like two turtles on a rock, talked about the days not so long ago when they played baseball with an oar handle on the Horse Lot and tried to scrounge up a nickel for the movies.

Joe didn't step out much at night in those days. He was content to sit around the modest, comfortable DiMaggio living room, filled with mementos of his days with the Seals and his great year with the Yankees. On the mantel, in the place of honor, stood the trophy he won as Most Valuable Player in the Coast League; on the tables stood ashtrays, gifts from friends and fans, engraved with their good wishes.

The radio he listened to was a gift from a group of San Francisco fans; the scrapbook his mother leafed through idly was a gift from a local admirer who had been following his career daily in the San Francisco newspapers.

Some nights Joe would go bowling or take in a movie with his friend Frank LaRocca, who pitched semipro ball when Joe was still a scatter-armed infielder. And to the surprise and amusement of his family, sometimes he'd get up at dawn and join his brothers Mike and Tom in their crab-fishing ventures, or fish for striped bass in San Francisco Bay with his new North Beach friends.

It was a quiet winter for Joe. Maybe it was true, as one sportswriter joked in print, that Joe was just resting for the battle that was sure to come with the Yankee management over his 1937 salary. Salary hassles were to mark most of Joe's years with the Yankees.

The fact that he'd been a raw rookie breaking in hadn't deterred Joe DiMaggio from being a holdout at contract

time the year before; now that he was a full-fledged
Yankee it was rather expected by the front office that Joe
would hold out again. And he did. He was offered a fif-
teen-thousand-dollar contract to sign, an increase of better
than five thousand dollars over the year before. But Joe
wanted twenty thousand dollars.

While his teammates were getting in shape in Florida,
Joe fought the salary war from his home in San Francisco.
Finally, in the middle of March, Joe came to terms at seventeen thousand dollars, just about twice his freshman
salary.

Again, however, Joe developed an injury. Almost
as soon as he reported for spring training he noticed a
twinge in his arm when he threw hard. He kept telling
himself that the warmer weather would straighten it out,
but despite baking treatments and exposure to the hot
Florida sun, the pain did not leave him. Finally Joe had to
be benched, and through the northward exhibition swing
he pinch-hit only, getting six hits in twelve trips to the
plate.

In Knoxville, Tennessee, a local doctor told Joe he had
an infected tooth and enlarged tonsils. Either, or both,
the doctor told him, could be the cause of his arm troubles. So for the second straight year Joe was sent on
ahead to New York to right himself. Out came the tooth
and the tonsils.

It wasn't until April 19 that Joe was able to report back
to the ball club, and on May 1 he broke into the lineup
again. His first day back he got three hits and won the
game for the Yankees, but he wasn't too happy. In the
locker room after the game he sought out Lefty Gomez.

"I don't know, Lefty," he said morosely, "I'm beginning
to get the feeling I'm jinxed or something."

"Jinxed?" Gomez looked at him in astonishment. "He gets three hits and he thinks he's jinxed! I should be jinxed like that!"

"No, that's not it." Joe shook his head. "I mean, look, something's always happening to me. In San Francisco I hurt my knee. Last year I almost burned my foot off, and now that arm got me. It worries me sometimes."

"Aw, go on, kid," Gomez said. "Look at you. You're healthy as a horse. These things happen to everybody. When you're playing baseball, something's always turning up to keep you out for a while. Me, I get blisters on my fingers. Or a cold in my arm." He shrugged. "Don't worry, kid, you always come back strong, don't you?"

"Yeah," Joe admitted. "But I don't know. One of these days some darn injury's going to ruin me for good," he said.

The Yankees of 1937 were practically a carbon copy of the Bronx Bombers of 1936. And they had added another big bat to their version of Murderers' Row—Tommy Henrich. On May 23 they took over first place from the Tigers and were never headed.

Free of aches and pains, DiMaggio was having another great year. In July he hit a home run into the left-field bleacher section at Yankee Stadium that veteran observers said was longer than anything Babe Ruth had ever hit. And how he fielded! Charlie Gehringer, the great Detroit Tiger slugger, remarked in disgust one afternoon after he'd been twice robbed of extra-base hits by Joe, "The only way to get a hit in Yankee Stadium is to hit the ball where DiMaggio can't get to it. And that seems to be only in the grandstand!"

The All-Star game that year was virtually the Yankees vs. the National League. McCarthy managed the American League and chose DiMaggio again, plus Gomez, Rolfe, Dickey, and Gehrig. The Yankee-led American Leaguers romped in the winners, 8–3, and Joe had the satisfaction of getting his first All-Star game hit, a single off Dizzy Dean.

In August, with the Yankees well on their way to the pennant again, Joe paid a visit to another champion slugger, Joe Louis, the heavyweight champion of the world. Louis was in training at Pompton Lakes, New Jersey, for his coming fight with British challenger Tommy Farr.

The two sports greats, silent men both, shook hands solemnly. "Hi, Joe," said DiMaggio. "I just wanted to come by and say hello."

Louis nodded. "Glad you did, Joe. How you been?"

DiMaggio nodded. "Okay, Joe. How you think you'll do with Farr?"

"I think I'll win, Joe," said the boxing champion.

"I hear Farr butts a lot," Joe retorted.

"I got a hard head," Louis chuckled. "He ain't gonna push me around."

"You think you'll knock him out?" DiMaggio asked.

Louis shrugged. "I'm gonna try hard. If I lick him in one round, I lick him in one round. If I lick him in ten rounds, I lick him in ten rounds. I do like you do. I try my best."

When DiMaggio left, Louis turned to the sportswriters. "Ain't he a nice fellow?" he said. "You know, when I see the Yankees play my Tigers," added the champ, who was from Detroit, "I say I hope DiMaggio gets a hit. He's the only ballplayer I root for, when he plays against my Tigers. That boy has class, plenty of class," said Louis. "I sure wish I could be a ballplayer like Joe DiMaggio."

14

For a young man just turned twenty-three, Joe DiMaggio was sitting on top of the baseball world. After a visit back home with the folks, here he was back in New York in January, settled down in a comfortable suite at the Mayflower Hotel, holding court to a roomful of baseball writers. A visitor, recalling how Joe looked when he first reported to the Yankees two short years ago, couldn't help noticing the change that had taken place. Still solemn at times, yet more relaxed, DiMaggio had taken on big-city airs. His clothes were expensive; he was just a bit more at ease.

"What are your plans in town, Joe?" asked one of the writers.

Joe blew out a cloud of cigarette smoke. "Well, I came in to see the Jim Braddock-Tommy Farr fight and I'll be rooting for Jimmy. I have to go to Philadelphia; the writers there are giving me a plaque on the twenty-fifth, and you fellows are giving me a dinner on the thirtieth. And I want to thank you now for naming me 'Player of the Year.'"

"Nobody else but you deserved it, Joe," a writer said.

"How's the restaurant business, Joe?" another put in.

DiMaggio had opened a seafood restaurant on the waterfront in San Francisco when he went home after the World Series.

"Doing great," Joe said. "We call the place DiMaggio's Grotto. It kept me pretty busy—shaking hands with customers and counting the take." He laughed. "My brother Tom manages the place and when little Dom isn't playing with the Seals he helps Tom."

"How about that romance supposed to be brewing on the Coast?" came the next question.

Joe blushed a little. "You're wrong there. There's no romance, never has been."

"What was the name of the girl—Dorothy Arnold, or something?" the writer persisted teasingly. "Ever hear of her, Joe? You know, she's an actress and very good-looking."

"Sure I know her," DiMaggio answered shortly. "But there's nothing to the rumor. Who started it, anyway?" he demanded angrily.

The writers decided to switch the subject. "How much you going to ask for as your 1938 salary?"

"I don't know," Joe answered. "I think it would be good business for me to see what they offer before I say anything. Don't you think so?"

"Well," the probing continued, "do you think Colonel Ruppert or Ed Barrow will invite you down for a talk while you're here?"

"I don't know," Joe returned again. "They know where to find me if they want me. I'm not going to look them up first."

A few eyebrows were raised at this. It seemed to be rather brash talk for a youngster.

As a matter of fact, Joe finally did seek out the Yankee

management. After the New York Baseball Writers' dinner on January 30, when he still hadn't been approached with a contract, he went to Colonel Jacob Ruppert, the brewery magnate, who then owned the Yankees.

After brief pleasantries, the two men got down to business.

"Colonel Ruppert," Joe said firmly, "I think I should get forty thousand dollars this year."

Ruppert's mouth flew open. He had the reputation of being a generous employer, not addicted to haggling with the men on the team when it came to a few thousand dollars. But this was too much. He looked steadily at DiMaggio. Joe's expression was serious, stubbornly set.

"I'll give you twenty-five thousand dollars. That's five thousand more than I figured on when you walked in here."

Joe shook his head. "No deal. Forty thousand. No less."

Colonel Ruppert looked at him curiously. "I wonder where you got the notion you're worth forty thousand dollars to the Yankees or to any baseball club. You're just a kid, you've only played a couple of years."

Joe shrugged. "That's what I figure I'm worth."

Ruppert stood up. "Joe, I want to tell you something. You've been getting some bad advice. Babe Ruth played for me a long time before he made that kind of money, and he was the greatest home-run hitter of all time. Lou Gehrig played with me for more than ten years before he got that kind of money. Now I'm telling you, DiMaggio, you're not Ruth, and you're no Gehrig—not yet, anyhow, but if that's the way you feel you can go back home right now 'cause I'm not paying you forty thousand dollars, or anything near that kind of money."

Joe got up from his chair and walked to the door. "I'll be in San Francisco if you change your mind," he said.

When he had gone Colonel Ruppert sat down again, sighing wearily. "Somebody," he said aloud, "somebody has been giving that young man some very bad advice."

That was the way most observers began to view it, too. At first DiMaggio's holdout wasn't considered seriously, no more so than were his holdouts the first two seasons. Hardly anyone thought he was serious in his demand for forty thousand dollars.

But the Yankees reported to St. Petersburg for spring training and still DiMaggio stayed home. Since the meeting with Colonel Ruppert, neither man had communicated with the other.

Possibly as an expression of the changing times, or possibly a mere indication that Joe had jumped the gun by holding out after so short a period in the big leagues, public sentiment was almost wholly against him.

Now the newspapers, the fans, and the Yankee players themselves became concerned. Some of the Yankee stars became angry. They thought Joe should be with them, getting into shape, instead of sitting around back in San Francisco. Many sportswriters took Joe to task for his unreasonable demands, and they berated Joe in their columns. This time they said it was DiMaggio who was wrong.

"DiMaggio may be an outstanding player," one wrote, "but apparently he's got the idea that he's the greatest thing to come out of the bushes since the history of baseball. Twenty-five thousand dollars is a lot of money for a player with just two years of major-league ball behind him."

"Who does DiMaggio think he is?" another columnist scorched him. "Babe Ruth? Not yet he isn't. He better report to spring training in a hurry, or he may not even make the team."

The weeks went by and DiMaggio remained in San Francisco. Criticism of his stand grew. With the Yankees looking bad in their spring exhibition games, the sportswriters flocked to Colonel Ruppert to see if he might give in to Joe's demands. But the colonel seemed even more insistent that DiMaggio sign for twenty-five thousand dollars.

"I think twenty-five thousand dollars is a very good salary for DiMaggio," he said. "He made seventeen thousand dollars last year. I think an eight-thousand-dollar increase is a generous one."

"You think there's a chance Joe'll come down a little and you'll come up a little in your offer?" Ruppert was asked.

"That's my final offer," Ruppert shook his head. "Not a penny more. I like to win ball games, but I'll pay DiMaggio only twenty-five thousand dollars even if the Yankees finish last without him."

That same night Joe Gould, manager of Jimmy Braddock, heavyweight boxer and close friend of DiMaggio's, phoned him long distance.

"You hear from the Yankees?"

"No," Joe said, "and they won't hear from me, either."

"You know, Joe," Gould said, "I've been thinking the past few days. If you don't open the season with the Yankees you may be seriously affecting your future. This is the year for you to really get going. You're in good shape, you've got a chance to break all kinds of records and put yourself in the position where the Yankees'll have to pay you the money you want. But if you miss a lot of games, you could get in wrong with the press and the fans."

Joe was silent a moment. "How's the weather in New York?" he asked finally.

"Great," Gould replied. "Perfect baseball weather."

"I wish I was there now," Joe said.

"A lot of people around here wish you were, too."

The next morning Ed Barrow received a telegram from DiMaggio. "Your terms accepted. Leave at 3:40 P.M. today. Arrive seven-thirty Saturday morning."

When DiMaggio reported to Yankee Stadium on April 23, he learned that the Yankees were docking him one hundred and sixty-two dollars for each day he was out of the regular lineup. His salary would not start until he was in shape to play, a condition that Manager Joe McCarthy would ascertain.

Some of the sportswriters, however, queried DiMaggio on a possible bonus to offset this loss in pay.

"If I'm supposed to get a bonus somebody's keeping it a big secret," he said. "As far as I know I won't even get my twenty-five thousand dollars."

"You sorry you held out so long, Joe?"

"I still think I'm worth more than I'm getting," he retorted. "But—" he shrugged his shoulders.

Joe McCarthy, the Yankee pilot, strolled up to the group. He still hadn't talked to DiMaggio. He stuck out his hand.

"How do you feel?" he asked. "You look like you've been sitting under an umbrella all winter."

"I'll be ready in no time," Joe said. "I had a tan for a while when I worked out with the Seals in California, but

I lost it hanging around my restaurant. I'll be okay, Joe, don't worry. I want to get a bat in my hands."

When the Yankees took their batting practice, Joe grabbed a bat and stood in to take his cuts. Red Ruffing, the Yankee ace, was pitching practice that day. Joe swung easily at the first few serves, then set himself and blasted Ruffing's next offering high and deep into the left-field stands. He stroked several more pitches cleanly into the deep outfield stretches of Yankee Stadium, then lifted another drive into the left-field seats.

Manager McCarthy grinned. "That guy could get out of bed on New Year's morning and hit home runs," he said.

But when the game against the Washington Senators began, Joe was on the bench. He sat there the next day, too. And the next. And when the Yankees left the Stadium for Philadelphia he rode the bench again. He took long hours of extra hitting practice, till his hands were raw and blistered from gripping the bat. And he had the batting coaches hitting fungos out to the outfield every morning before the regular practice session started.

In Washington, finally, on April 30, McCarthy put Joe into the lineup. He had missed the first twelve games of the season, and lost almost two thousand dollars of his pay. Joe was soon to learn, however, that this was the least of his losses. He had also lost a lot of friends.

15

Joe DiMaggio couldn't believe his ears. He stood there in the batter's box at Washington's Griffith Stadium, his bat cocked, and the boos and jeers from the stands cascaded down on him. A good ballplayer often gets some mild hooting from the stands in an enemy ball park, but this, Joe realized at once, was not that kind of good-natured booing. And it stung.

But he squared his shoulders and stood in at the plate. Let them boo, he thought to himself. I'll show them. And he cracked the first pitch on a line to left field for a single. The boos grew louder. "Aw, you were lucky, DiMaggio," a fan shouted at him as he led off first base. In the third inning, after he grounded out, a shower of paper cups joined the jeers from the stands as he trotted along the first-base line on the way back to the bench.

In center field, too, when the Yankees were on defense, the fans joined in a chorus of jeers and boos. And in the sixth inning an unfortunate accident started the fans howling still louder. The Senators had two men on and two out in their half of the sixth. Taft Wright, the Senators' batter, hit a looping fly ball back of second base.

DiMaggio raced in for it. Myril Hoag, playing right field, came over to try for it, and Joe Gordon, who had come up that year to replace Tony Lazzeri at second base, drove back for the tricky ball. All three men reached the same spot at the same time. Hoag managed to make the catch and hold the ball as the three men collided, but Gordon was knocked over by DiMaggio and had to be carried from the field on a stretcher.

It was just one of those accidents that happen every once in a while in a ball game, but the fans tore into Joe as if he'd run Gordon down deliberately.

From Washington the Yankees journeyed to Philadelphia and then to Boston. The story was the same in both cities. From the first inning until the game was over, the fans booed DiMaggio's every move on the field. And he was playing great ball, too. The Yankees had been floundering so far that year, but when Joe stepped into the lineup they began to move. A new spirit took over the team as DiMaggio's bat flashed and the base hits started bouncing off the walls of the ball parks.

The Yankees finally came home to Yankee Stadium, and DiMaggio was hitting at a fantastic .500 clip. Well, Joe thought, as he got into his suit in the locker room that morning, things ought to be different here. Back in friendly territory now, it'll be great to hear friendly cheers from the crowd for a change.

But his heart chilled when he came out into the sunshine and took his pregame practice. His appearance on the field had always been the signal for a demonstration of hero worship by the fans. This time he was met with a stony silence and here and there a catcall as he took his swings in the batting-practice cage.

The game was about to start, and the Yankees sat in the

dugout listening to the public-address announcer giving the lineups. "Batting in No. 4 position, playing center field, Joe DiMaggio. . . ." At the announcement, a great chorus of boos broke out in the stands, so loud they drowned out the voice on the loudspeaker. The noise continued in an unrelenting wave. In the dugout, DiMaggio hung his head and choked back the tears.

The other Yankee players shifted restlessly on the bench. They were angry at the fans and sorry for Joe, but they didn't quite know how to express their feelings. All they could do was pat Joe encouragingly on the back as the team took the field for the start of the game.

Two men were out, with Tommy Henrich on first base, when DiMaggio came to bat in the first inning. The boos began again. Joe bit his lip and set himself determinedly. There was only one way to answer back, to get the fans on his side again. He lashed out at the first pitch and sent it screaming on a line to left-center field, up the alley between the outfielder for extra bases. Henrich whirled around third and headed for the plate, Joe raced around second and sped for third as the throw came in from the outfield. He saw the third baseman set himself for the throw-in, the third-base coach signaling him to slide. Joe hurled himself through the air, feet first, and slid into third in a cloud of dust. He was safe with a triple!

Joe called time and stood up, dusting the dirt from his uniform. A couple of faint cheers came from the stands but they were quickly drowned by a cascade of jeers. The Athletics' third baseman shook his head and looked at DiMaggio. "They're sure on you, DiMag," he said. "I guess it's because you're always holding out for more money?"

Joe shrugged. "Let 'em boo," he said. "They pay to get

in, they got a right to boo me if they want to." But his lips quivered and his voice trembled as he spoke.

In the fourth inning he hit into a force play, and as he led off first base the fans in the seats along the base line began to ride him. "Hey, Babe Ruth," a voice jeered, "how about a home run next time up, eh? Or ain't you gettin' paid enough to hit home runs?" The crowd in hearing range laughed at the taunt. When DiMaggio acted as if he hadn't heard, the riding got rougher.

"Hey, Joe," yelled another voice, "what're ya gonna do with your first million? Buy the Yankees?"

Day after day, the boos and the taunts fell about Joe's ears. He endured them silently. But his teammates knew how he was suffering, and they suffered with him. Many of them had never been friendly toward him since his surliness and aloofness baffled them, but he won new respect from the veteran Yankees for his silence now.

The newspapers, hostile to Joe during his holdout, came back to his side. To a man, the sportswriters blasted the fans for their bad sportsmanship. "Joe's salary disagreement with the Yankees is over," one wrote. "And no matter how we or the fans felt about his stand during the argument is now beside the point. Joe is back and he's playing his heart out, as he always did. It's incredible and grossly unfair for the fans to boo Joe the way they have been at the Stadium."

"The unwarranted abuse of Joe DiMaggio is a shameful act," wrote another in a blistering attack on the fans. "If a large percentage of Yankee patrons are bent on destroying his ambition and usefulness to the club, they're making a good start."

In his eagerness to surpass himself, Joe began to press

hard. The day before, he had gotten only one single during a double-header with the Cleveland Indians. He was tense and unsure, trying too hard to win back the fans—and he looked bad.

The Yankee players tried kidding him out of his slump. "Hey, Joe," Crosetti said to him one day, "I think maybe you better wear a catcher's mask on the back of your head when you're in the field. One of those characters in the stands is gonna throw a bottle at you someday."

Joe smiled wryly, and the Yankees soon gave up that angle on cheering him up.

By the middle of July the Yankees were in first place. Cleveland made another run at them, but with only two games separating the clubs at one point, DiMaggio stopped the Indians' chance.

It was a double-header at Yankee Stadium. Bob Feller pitched the first game for Cleveland, against Monte Pearson. An Indian sweep would put them percentage points ahead of the Yankees. Feller, his blazing fast ball under control that day, had the Yankees behind 2–0 into the last of the ninth.

Crosetti opened the Yankees' last chance with a single—only the fourth hit off Feller. Rolfe popped to short, but Henrich walked. Up to the plate strode DiMaggio. He had walked, popped up, and struck out so far that day. A torrent of jeers greeted him as he stepped in to face Feller.

Bob took a look at the runners, stretched, then burned a fast ball through. Joe swung and missed. A fast curve spun outside, ball one. Another fast ball down the middle, and Joe swung and missed again, strike two. A slow curve, inside, and the count was two balls and two strikes.

Feller took a deep breath, looked back at the runners, stretched, and came down with everything he had on a blistering fast ball. Joe swung—and there was a clean "thwock" as bat met ball. Feller took one look over his shoulder and his body sagged in defeat. He watched disconsolately as the ball sailed on a rising line into the left-field stands for a home run—and the ball game. The Yankees won, 3–2!

That broke Cleveland's back, and the Yankees went on to romp home in the second game of the double-header, 13–4. Joe's contribution to this effort was a pair of doubles and a walk, two runs scored, and four driven in. The Indians never recovered from the beatings, finally slipping to third place behind Boston.

Suddenly and magically, the booing stopped. While there seemed to be no sudden reason why the fans stopped reviling him, it was easily explainable. Sportswriter Bob Cooke of the New York *Herald Tribune*, noting the change in the fans' attitude, summed it up one day.

"It's pretty hard to hold a grudge against a guy who takes abuse without complaint, public or private, and continues to play the kind of ball DiMaggio has been playing. Even the most prejudiced fan must see by now that Joe is a great player, with plenty of heart."

On September 18 the Yankees clinched their third straight pennant. DiMaggio, despite his late start and troubles, led the team in batting with a mark of .324. He hit 32 home runs, 32 doubles, and 13 triples, batting in 140 runs and scoring 129 himself.

Though the Yankees had won the pennant handily, beating the Red Sox by 9½ games, they had loafed

through the last 2 weeks of the season. The Chicago
Cubs, on the other hand, had brought home the National
League pennant with a great stretch run and were given
a good chance to beat the Yankees in the World Series.

Another thing was worrying some of the Yankees. Lou
Gehrig, the great "Iron Horse," hadn't played well the latter part of the season. For the first time since 1925 he had
hit less than .300—he hit .295—and he wasn't looking his
old self around first base. Unknown to everyone, the in-
sidious disease that was to take Lou shortly thereafter had
begun its deadly work.

Behind Red Ruffing, the Yankees took the Series
opener, 3–1. The fading Dizzy Dean, who had been sold
to the Cubs that season, started the second game, facing
Lefty Gomez. Dizzy Dean didn't have much any longer;
the fast ball was gone, but he was game—and smart. Instead of fogging the ball through the way he did in the
old days, he fed the Yankees a sneaky curve and lots of
soft pitches. The Bronx Bombers were so eager to blast
Dean's dinky pitches that they either popped up or
topped easy grounders. When the Yanks came to bat in
the eighth, Dean had them, 3–2. But a pitcher needed
more than head and heart to beat the powerful Yankee
slugging crew.

Selkirk opened the Yankee attack with a single. Dean,
pitching with his head and heart, forced Gordon and
Hodges on two successive off-speed curves that were easy
put-outs. But with two out, Crosetti hit a home run to give
the Yankees a one-run lead. Dean struck Rolfe out to end
the inning with the Yankees just one run ahead, the Cubs
were still in the game. But in the ninth inning Henrich
singled and DiMaggio slammed one of Dean's soft curves

over the left-field wall. That was all for Dean, and the Yankees won, 6–3.

The scene now shifted to the Stadium, and the Yankees continued their overpowering domination of the National Leaguers. The Cubs scored first, in the fifth inning, but the Yankees came back with two runs in their half. Then, in the sixth, DiMaggio started the attack that sewed up the game. He singled to left to open the inning. Gehrig followed with a single, Selkirk walked, Gordon singled, and two runs were in for a 4–1 Yankee lead. With Monte Pearson on the mound for them, that's all they needed, winning the game, 5–2.

The Yankees made it four in a row next day for their sweep of the World Series, and their third straight world championship, a new record. The score was 8–3, but it was a lot closer than that until DiMaggio again opened things up. The Yankees were holding onto a slim 4–3 lead in their half of the eighth. With one out, DiMaggio singled, then the roof fell in. By the time the rally was over, four runs had crossed the plate to put the game and the World Series on ice.

The single was Joe's fourth hit of the Series, giving him a .267 average for the four games. But each one of his blows—three singles and a home run—came in a pinch, starting a rally or clinching a tight game.

All in all, it was a good season statistically for DiMaggio. But he always remarked in his later years that 1938 was a season he'd like to forget. The memory of the booing fans lingered with him for a long time and it was to haunt him for many years afterward.

16

Love and a kind of level-headed maturity seemed to come simultaneously to Joe DiMaggio early in 1939. In February he told a reporter for United Press that he would be asking the Yankee management for a five-thousand-dollar raise. But, he added, this time he would not let a few thousand dollars interfere with his spring training.

"I've learned my lesson," Joe said. "I'm acting on my own this year, no advisers. I'm tired of getting behind schedule and reporting out of shape. This year I'll be in Florida on time and ready to start with the rest of the team on Opening Day, something I've never done since I joined the Yankees."

Joe's new attitude was probably induced by a number of factors. One undoubtedly was the death several months before of Colonel Jake Ruppert, president of the Yankees. Ruppert, a sharp businessman, was easier to deal with around contract time, but Ed Barrow, who replaced Ruppert, had no such weakness, as Joe knew from his experience with Barrow the year before. Getting a raise out of Barrow, Joe realized, might force another holdout. This he meant to avoid at all costs.

Second, there was the matter of Dorothy Arnold. This was the girl Joe denied knowing more than casually back in 1937. But a romance was blossoming. She, a movie bit player at the time, had met Joe while she was making her first movie in a studio in Astoria, Long Island. Joe had been persuaded to appear briefly in the movie himself.

Now, two years later, the romance was indeed a serious one. But Joe was not quite ready to make any announcements. His decision to get into shape early and have a good year was part of his plan for the future, however. "Two can't live as cheaply as one," Joe confided to one of his San Francisco friends. "I'm going to need a good year so I can ask for a raise and get it next year."

True to his word, Joe reported to spring training with the rest of the Yankees. And his appearance made a world of difference to the team. They played together as a solid unit from the beginning. When they finally left St. Petersburg and started their preseason exhibition tour, they were ready to sweep through the league. In the meantime, they tried their muscle out on some minor-league competition.

The first stop for the Yankees was New Orleans, where they played the Pelicans of the Class AA Southern Association in a three-game series. DiMaggio slammed out two homers, four doubles, a triple, and a single as the Yankees swept through the New Orleans team, then swept North for the championship season.

On the momentum started in the exhibition games, the Yankees roared right into first place when the regular season began. Two weeks later, DiMaggio announced his engagement to Dorothy Arnold. "But we won't get married until the fall," he said. "I have a long baseball season ahead of me. We've known each other for two years; I guess we can wait a little while longer to get married."

April was a fateful month all around for DiMaggio and the Yankees. It was the morning of April 29, and with a night game scheduled at Yankee Stadium with the Washington Senators, the writers were looking for a story for the early editions.

DiMaggio was always good copy—that is, if he could be made to talk. This morning he was willing. "Joe," Max Kase, sports editor of the *Journal-American*, asked him, "what's the one goal you'd like to achieve in baseball?"

DiMaggio answered promptly. "I want to get more base hits than anyone in the league. I want to win the batting crown."

"How about home runs? Wouldn't you like to hit sixty-one and beat Ruth's record?"

Joe shook his head. "I'm not going for homers. I just want to hit that ball, get on base as often as I can, and drive in runs."

Joe's ambition looked as if it might well be realized that season. He was hitting .409 and was in great shape. That night, however, misfortune struck Joe DiMaggio again.

In the third inning, with the Yankees behind, 3–1, Bill Estalella drove a line drive into center field. DiMaggio started after the ball. He slipped and his spikes caught in the dirt, throwing him on his back. He lay there, rolling back and forth in terrible pain, while Estalella ran out a triple.

As soon as the play was over, Dr. Robert Walsh, the Yankees' physician, and trainer Doc Painter hurried to DiMaggio's side.

It was fully five minutes before Joe was able to rise and be helped off the field. He was rushed to St. Elizabeth's Hospital, where X rays showed badly torn muscles above the right ankle. "DiMaggio'll be out for about ten days," Dr. Walsh told reporters. But he had underestimated the damage this time.

With the opening of the season no one could figure out just what was the matter with Lou Gehrig. He had—for him—rather a bad year in 1938. He had made a good start, but a terrific slump had gripped him soon after the teams had passed the halfway mark. Nothing he could do would free him of it. His average skidded. There were fewer home runs. Because of his fine start Lou wound up with 29 homers and a .295 batting average. It was the first time since 1925 he had failed to hit .300 or better.

Now in the spring of 1939, he couldn't hit, and he couldn't field. He was slow getting down for a ball, slow getting up, slow covering the bag, slow getting the ball away. Now and then one of the sportswriters asked McCarthy a question about him. When he did, Joe shook it off or answered evasively.

Lou had come to the Yankees directly from Columbia University in 1923, where his towering drives were being compared to Babe Ruth's. Gehrig played briefly with the Yankees in 1923, but was sent to Hartford for a year of experience. Brought back in 1924, Lou was again sent down to Hartford, where he slowly began to assert himself at the plate. Brought back late in the season, Lou played well. In 1927, the year Babe Ruth smashed out a record-breaking total of sixty home runs, Gehrig smashed out forty-seven and batted for a .373 average as the Yankees coasted home to win both the pennant and the World Series.

During the ensuing dozen years, Columbia Lou Gehrig became, next to Babe Ruth, the most feared batsman in the major leagues. Together Ruth and Gehrig became the most feared one-two punch in baseball history.

Year after year Gehrig a huge, good-natured, quiet giant, challenged Babe Ruth for the home-run championship of the American League. In 1931 Lou blasted out forty-six home runs to tie Ruth for the championship. In 1934 Lou still improving at the bat and at first base, finally won the home-run derby by slugging out forty-nine four-base wallops.

In 1935, Babe Ruth slowly slipped into the twilight of his career, and Gehrig became the undisputed slugging star of the New York Yankees.

But now, in the spring of 1939, there was something radically wrong with Lou. And by April 30 Lou looked so bad in the field and at bat that McCarthy obviously was waiting for him to take himself out of the lineup. He had played eight games when on the night of April 30 the team left for Detroit. Since the next day was an off day, McCarthy stopped off at his home in Buffalo. When he reached Detroit on the morning of May 2, Lou spoke to him:

"Joe, I'm benching myself."

McCarthy was silent for a moment, and then:

"Why?"

"For the good of the team," Lou said. "I just can't seem to get going, and nobody has to tell me how I've been and how much of a drawback I've been to the team. I've been thinking: The time has come for me to quit."

"Quit? You don't have to quit. Take a rest for a week or so, and maybe you'll feel all right again."

Lou shook his head and told Joe the story of the last play he had made—the final play in the game at the Stadium on the thirteenth. A ball hit between the pitcher's box and first base, and Johnny Murphy fielding it and tossing it to him, just in time to make the put-out and Murphy saying, as they hurried from the field,

"Nice play, Lou."

"I knew then," Lou said, "that it was time to quit."

"All right, Lou," Joe said. "Take a rest. I'll put Babe Dahlgren on first base today. But remember, that's your position—and whenever you want it back, just you walk out and take it."

For the first time since June 1, 1925, Gehrig sat in the dugout that day as the Yankees took the field. His magnificent string of 2,130 consecutive games had been broken. The story flashed across the country, hit the headlines on every sports page . . . on every radio broadcast . . . over every loudspeaker in a ball park that day.

GEHRIG BENCHED   DAHLGREN ON FIRST BASE FOR
                YANKEES

That ended the greatest streak in baseball—2,130 consecutive games played—and a whole nation was saddened as the curtain rang down on one of the most beloved heroic figures in baseball history.

Despite the absence of DiMaggio and Gehrig, the Yankees continued at a hot pace, and when Joe returned to the lineup it was all over for the rest of the clubs. At the end of August, the Yankees went on their final swing through the West. They won ten out of twelve games on the road trip, and what DiMaggio didn't do to wreck the enemy pitchers, Charlie Keller, the rookie wonder, made sure to do.

Joe not only hit in every game during that western swing, he also got twenty-seven hits in fifty-three at-bats for a fantastic .509 average. He hit five homers and batted in twenty-eight runs during those twelve games. The final game of the tour in Cleveland proved a fitting climax to his one-man show.

Bob Feller was on the mound for Cleveland, seeking his twentieth win, but DiMaggio had been Bob's nemesis ever since the pitcher had broken into the major leagues. And this game was no exception. In the third inning, with two men on base, Joe drove Feller's fast ball into left center for a two-run triple. In the next inning he sent Feller to the showers with his second hit, a single that again scored two runs.

Still Joe wasn't through. The Yankees led, going into the last half of the seventh inning, 7–2. But Monte Pearson faltered and the Tribe broke loose to tie it up, then flash ahead, 8–7.

In the Yankee half of the eighth inning, DiMaggio strode to the plate to face the Indians' relief hurler, Al Milnar. The Cleveland ace got across a strike—and that's all. DiMaggio rocketed the next serve 430 feet to right-center for his second triple of the day, and his fifth and sixth runs batted in. Joe trotted in on Keller's fly-out, and the Yankees won it, 11–8.

When the Yankees returned back home to the Stadium, DiMaggio made one of the greatest catches in history. The great Tiger first baseman Hank Greenberg drove a long, high drive 450 feet to straightaway center field. At the crack of the bat, DiMaggio turned his back and raced to deep center field. The ball was hit so high and so far that DiMaggio stopped and turned, judged the flight of the ball, ran on some more, stopped, turned, and got his bearings again, then raced as far as he could go and caught the ball finally on the dead run, over his shoulder.

Observers said it was a fantastic thing, the way Joe tracked that ball down. One sportswriter turned to the man at his side and said, "I just lost one of my all-time idols. I always thought Tris Speaker was the greatest center fielder of all time, but this DiMaggio beats Speaker."

Despite his month out of the lineup and a damaged leg, Joe did realize his ambition! He won the batting championship with a .381 average, the highest mark he was ever to reach in his career. He also hit 30 home runs and batted in 126 runs in the 120 games he played. Baseball fans were not surprised when, after the World Series, Joe was named the American League's Most Valuable Player by the sportswriters.

The 1939 World Series was practically a repeat of the '38 Series, only this time the Cincinnati Reds instead of the Chicago Cubs were victims of a four-game Yankee sweep. With this world championship, the Yankees became the only team to that time to win four straight World Series.

The Yanks' Charlie Keller was the big gun of the Series, hitting .438, and DiMaggio was the only other Yankee to hit better than .300, with a .313 average.

It was one of DiMaggio's finest years. He had won the batting championship, was named the league's Most Val-

uable Player, and *The Sporting News,* the national baseball newspaper, named him the Major League Player of
the Year. And then, with baseball over for the year, Joe
returned to San Francisco and on November 19 married
Dorothy Arnold.

The Yankees, of course, figured to have a letdown
sometime, but the next year might not have been the year
had DiMaggio been in the lineup from the start. Unfortu-
nately, this was another of Joe's "jinx" seasons. He reported to spring training in good shape, happier than ever
before, feeling like "one of the boys" now that he had his
wife in camp like many of the Yankee veterans. He got
into playing shape rapidly and looked all set to start the
season, until the afternoon before Opening Day at the
Stadium.

That last game of the exhibition season was against the
Dodgers at Ebbets Field, and the Yankees were winning,
5–3, in the ninth inning. DiMaggio, first up in the inning,
rapped Hugh Casey for a hit to right center. It was only
an exhibition game but DiMaggio played as if they were
going after the pennant. He rounded first and scooted for
second. As the throw came in, he slid into the bag hard.
Everyone in the park saw at once that something had
happened to Joe's leg.

Joe was safe, but he lay writhing in agony at second
base. His spikes had caught in the base and his right knee
was badly twisted. DiMaggio's injuries always seemed
less serious than they really turned out to be. Just as before, it was predicted that he'd be back in action in a
week or ten days. But it wasn't until May 7, three weeks
later, that Joe started his first game of the 1940 regular

season. By this time, the Yankees were in last place and they couldn't seem to move. In July, DiMaggio finally started hitting, and the Yankees started going somewhere.

From July 4, Joe hit in twenty-three straight games, and the Yankees moved up to fifth place. But they had already lost forty-six games for the season, one more than they had lost in the entire season of 1939. And they were twelve games out of first place.

All of a sudden Joe's batting fell off. He couldn't buy a hit. Every ball was either popped up or was hit weakly on the ground. Up to that point he had been the only Yankee regular batting over .300. With Joe slumping, the Yankees battled to remain in the first division.

Nobody on the team could find what was causing the slump. It took an inexperienced eye to catch what was wrong. For it was Dorothy, Joe's wife, who solved the riddle.

One night at dinner in their apartment Dorothy spoke up.

"Joe," she said hesitantly, "I know this is something I shouldn't talk about perhaps, but I noticed something about you today at the game."

Joe looked up at her curiously. "What was it?"

"Well—" she still hesitated, for she knew how baseball players disliked having "experts" for wives.

"Go on, honey," Joe urged. "You can't be any more wrong than everyone else has been so far."

"I think I know what's wrong with your hitting," she said. "You know I always sit in the same seat every day, and always watch you from the same angle. Well, today I happened to notice that when you finished your swing, the No. 5 on your back is in a different position from what it used to be."

Joe looked at her for a moment, amazed. "I got it," he said. "That means that I've developed a hitch in my swing. I'll alter my stance a little and try to work it out tomorrow when I take batting practice. You call out to me when you see that old angle back on my number, right?"

That was the answer, apparently. Joe got three hits that next day and caught fire again. Once more he slammed runs across the plate in game after game, and the pennant race became a three-way affair among the Yankees, the Detroit Tigers, and the Cleveland Indians. The race for the batting crown, too, became a hot one, with Rip Radcliff of the Browns, Luke Appling of the White Sox, Ted Williams of the Red Sox, and Hank Greenberg of the Tigers batting it out with Joe.

DiMaggio's two hits on the last day of the season not only won the ball game for Ernie Bonham, it also earned Joe the batting crown for the second straight year. But it was this close: DiMaggio, .352; Luke Appling, .348; Ted Williams, .344; Rip Radcliff, .342; and Hank Greenberg and Barney McCosky of the Tigers, .340.

Joe was also fourth in the league in home runs, with 31, and second to Greenberg in runs batted in, with 133.

Only one circumstance spoiled Joe's season, aside from not winning the pennant, of course. In May he had been called on the carpet by baseball's Commissioner Kenesaw Mountain Landis regarding his association with Joe Gould. Back in 1938, it was rumored that Gould was managing DiMaggio's baseball career and was responsible for

Joe's long holdout. Though the boxing manager had convinced the Yankee management that he had nothing to do with it, stories continued to circulate that he was DiMaggio's silent manager and was getting 12 per cent of Joe's baseball salary.

Joe, however, denied that Gould, manager of former heavyweight champion Jim Braddock, received any part of his earnings. The Yankees were concerned only with the question of Gould's sharing DiMaggio's earnings as a player. "What money DiMaggio makes from outside sources," Manager McCarthy said, "is his own business. We are satisfied with Joe's denial that no one shares his baseball salary." That ended the inquiry.

Driving back to San Francisco that October, it seemed strange to Joe to be listening to the World Series on the radio. This was the first year since his arrival in New York that he and the Yankees were not participating in the annual classic.

"Ah, well," Joe sighed, "wait till next year."

Joltin' Joe DiMaggio is shown at a Boston hotel, reading the news accounts of his sensational home-run spree against the Boston Red Sox, June 30 and 31, 1949. In the game on the thirtieth (Tuesday), DiMag, who had not played a single game all year because of a heel injury, slugged a homer and two singles to beat the Sox. The next day (Wednesday), Joe belted two tremendous homers to again spur the Yanks to victory. It was one of the greatest individual performances in baseball history.

Yankees Selected for All-Star Game

Five members of the Yankees were named to the starting lineup of the annual All-Star game in 1949. Left to right: pitcher Vic Raschi, outfielder Tommy Henrich, Joe DiMaggio, pitcher Allie Reynolds, and catcher Yogi Berra.

At Yankee Stadium

Joe DiMaggio is shown stealing second base in a game between the Yankees and the St. Louis Browns on August 7, 1949. The throw to Eddie Pellagrini at second was wild; Joe advanced to third and later scored. The Yankees won, 20–2, while Joe drove out four base hits in the game.

It was Joe DiMaggio Day at Yankee Stadium, October 1,
1949, and a crowd of more than 65,000 fans turned out to
honor Joe.

Surrounded by members of his family: Dom DiMaggio (center fielder for the Boston Red Sox), brother Tom (rear), Momma DiMaggio, and Joe DiMaggio, Jr., Joe looks at one of the numerous awards given him on "his day." DiMaggio was gifted with dozens of trophies and presents.

Emcee Mel Allen introduces Joe DiMaggio at Joe DiMaggio Day at Yankee Stadium. Left rear: members of the Boston Red Sox, including Dom DiMaggio (Joe's brother).

Governor Thomas E. Dewey of New York presented a special World Series watch to Yankee star Joe DiMaggio at Yankee Stadium, April 21, 1950. The governor is shaking hands with DiMaggio, while Baseball Commissioner Happy Chandler and sportscaster Mel Allen look on at pregame ceremonies before a Yankee-Washington game.

Joe DiMaggio says hello to the great Willie Mays at a reception honoring Mays in New York City. Mays played for the New York Giants, the San Francisco Giants, and then finished out his career with the Mets. DiMaggio played out his entire baseball career from 1936 to 1951 with the New York Yankees.

17

The year 1941 was one of mixed blessings for DiMaggio and the Yankees. The ball club won the pennant again and beat the Brooklyn Dodgers in a hectic World Series. DiMaggio, with an average of .357, led the league in runs batted in with 125, and won the Most Valuable Player Award for the second time in three years, the Player of the Year Award for the second season in a row, and also the Athlete of the Year Award. His son Joe, Jr., was born in October, which gave him a bigger kick than all his awards combined.

But all the joys went down the drain when Japan bombed Pearl Harbor on December 7, 1941, and the United States entered World War II.

It was difficult to consider business as usual for the game of baseball with a war on, but President Roosevelt indicated that he hoped the game would continue as best it could. Transportation became a problem, and many of the players entered the armed forces, either by the draft or through voluntary enlistment.

A call from the Army didn't seem particularly imminent for DiMaggio, however. He was a married man with a child now, and also had a chronic ulcer condition that had been bothering him for the past several years. So when the spring of 1942 came around, DiMaggio found himself still a civilian, but involved again in a private war of his own with the Yankee management.

It was the usual story. After one of the greatest years in his career, Joe asked for an increase over the thirty-seven thousand dollars he had received the previous season, and after a lengthy battle he eventually settled his differences with Barrow. But with the war on, things somehow didn't seem the same to Joe. Ken Silvestri, Johnny Sturm, Charlie Stanceau, and Steve Peek went into the Army. Joe wasn't sure that his place was with the Yankees. He fretted and worried, wondering if he should enlist.

The pennant story, meanwhile, was the same. Until July, Cleveland and Boston made a fight out of it. Then the Yankees shot off by themselves. On August 30 Tommy Henrich enlisted in the Coast Guard, but the Yankees were still strong enough to walk away with the pennant. This may not have been one of the better Yankees teams— as critics pointed out—but they were better than anyone else in the league.

Yankee invincibility in the World Series was by now legendary, and no one saw any reason why this Series should be any different. The Yankees had loafed through September and were well rested. The Cardinals, on the other hand, had won the pennant only after a down-to-the-wire battle with the Dodgers. The Cardinals figured to be tired, played out.

And it looked just that way, too, up until the ninth inning of the first game. The Yankees, behind Red Ruffing, went into the ninth leading, 7–0. Then, with two out and

Walker Cooper on first, the Cardinals exploded. They knocked out Ruffing and had Spud Chandler on the ropes before Stan Musial grounded out with the bases loaded to end the game.

The Yankees won it, 7-4. But the Cardinals' sudden splurge had shaken their confidence, and had at the same time taken the edge off the Redbirds' nervousness. To everyone's amazement, including even their own, the Cardinals went on to sweep the next four straight to win the World Series.

In accomplishing the seemingly impossible, the Cards not only stopped the Yankees' world-championship string at five straight, they also won as many games—four—as eight previous National League clubs had been able to win from the Yankees since 1926.

In his downcast mood, DiMaggio blamed the Yankees' loss to the Cardinals partly on his own poor play. His "poor" play, however, was a .333 batting average. Still, he felt he could have done more, and he couldn't understand how some of the Yankees were able to joke in the dressing room after the final game. Losing a World Series was a calamity to Joe.

In January of 1943, Joe announced that he was enlisting in the Army. "I will return to baseball and the Yankees after the war, if I can still play," he said from his home in San Francisco. The following month he passed his physical, waived the privilege of a short leave, and headed for the Army reception center at Monterey, California.

Army food, however, didn't get along well with Joe's ulcers. As a matter of fact, many sportswriters had said in print that had DiMaggio been an ordinary civilian, he would have been rejected for military service on account of his ulcers. But the Army, they theorized, was afraid of accusations of "favoritism" toward professional athletes.

When Joe was assigned to the Army Air Force base at Santa Ana, California, his ulcers began kicking up immediately. The pain was so bad he couldn't sleep nights, but he let the condition drag on for weeks, afraid the other men would accuse him of malingering.

Finally he couldn't stand it any longer. He decided to go to the base hospital. That morning, however, he noticed that the pains had suddenly disappeared. With a feeling of relief he continued on duty.

Later, in Hawaii as a staff sergeant in the Air Force Special Services Division, he felt the ulcers acting up again. Finally, in the fall of 1944, the Army decided to ship Joe to the Thomas M. England General Hospital in Atlantic City, New Jersey, for extended treatment, rehabilitation, and reassignment. With a twenty-one-day "delay en route" furlough in his pocket, Joe came into New York for a visit with his now divorced wife, his son, who was now three years old, and his old friends.

The sportswriters, tracking him down, finally cornered him in Toots Shor's restaurant, a New York gathering place for many sporting-world figures and show-business personalities. Joe was a good friend of Shor's, despite the fact that the rotund restaurateur was a devoted Giant fan.

"Joe," the first question from a writer came to him, "is there anything significant to the fact that you're reporting to Atlantic City, where the Yankees will be doing their spring training in a few months?"

DiMaggio shook his head. "No. Just a coincidence."

"I understand you're due for a medical discharge soon," said the writer.

"No deal," Joe returned. "I haven't asked for one. I don't want one and I don't expect to get one. Not until the war's over, anyway."

"How's your condition, Joe?"

Joe looked down at himself. "Look at me." He smiled affably. "Skin and bones. I'm on a special diet, soft foods. I've lost about twenty-five pounds. But I got in about seventy-five games or so last summer in Hawaii, so I'm in better shape than a lot of players in the service."

"You think you might be back with the Yankees next year?"

"I doubt it," Joe said. "I'm sure I'll still be in the Army next year."

"You sure lost some good years being in the Army," commented a reporter.

Joe shrugged. "I was only thirty a couple of weeks ago. I should be good for a few more years when I get out." Then he grinned. "I hope."

"The Yanks sure could have used you this year. They came in third, you know."

"Yeah, too bad," Joe said. "But it's a mixed-up league now, with all the guys in the service."

"What's the bet the Yankees win the pennant the first year you come back, Joe?" a reporter said.

Joe smiled. "I wouldn't bet on that one. Besides, before we worry about winning the pennant, let's worry about winning the war."

The war was over now, and on a September afternoon in 1945 the last patchwork edition of the New York Yankees was going through the motions of finishing out a disappointing fourth-place-finish season. There were lots of open spaces in the Stadium grandstand, and the slim crowd was idly waiting for the day's game to get under way. There wasn't very much to get excited about.

Suddenly a burst of applause began in the mezzanine section. People stood up and craned their necks to see what it was all about. The applause turned into loud shouting, then excited chattering—and finally cheers and wave after wave of applause filled the Stadium.

Walking along the front row of the mezzanine, smiling acknowledgment to the fans, was a tall, dark-haired man in a neat gray double-breasted suit. An armed forces discharge button was in his lapel, and he looked suntanned and healthy. Holding onto his hand was a junior edition of the same man, a little boy with the same dark hair and dark eyes.

As he took his seat in the boxes overlooking the third-base line, Joe DiMaggio waved to the crowd, and little Joe DiMaggio waved, too. The fans in the section of stands called to the returned Air Force veteran, "H'ya, Joe!" "Glad to see you back, Joe!" "Nice to see you, Joe!"

Little Joe DiMaggio, who would be four the next month, turned to his famous father. "See, Daddy," he said, "everybody knows me."

In that third-base box, too, was the new Yankee boss, Larry MacPhail. And though the volatile MacPhail and his top slugger were to have many a disagreement later, this meeting, like all their early ones, was cordial. And two months later the Yankee president announced that DiMaggio had signed his contract for the 1946 season.

With the formalities of the contract signing out of the way, Joe settled down to an intensive training program to get himself back in shape for the next season. He showed up at the New York Athletic Club bright and early each morning, toiled earnestly on the cycling machine, ran around the track, and labored over weights and pulleys and rowing machines.

"I got to get down to St. Petersburg early this year," Joe said to a visitor at the gym. "Got to get my legs in shape. If your legs are in shape and your timing's right everything else will fall into line. After all, I haven't played a game of ball for a year and a half now. I got a lot of work cut out for me."

Under Larry MacPhail, the Yankees tried something new in the way of spring training. Figuring to get the jump on the other clubs, particularly with many out-of-shape veterans returned to all the teams, MacPhail got the Yankees down to the Panama Canal Zone in February. There, under the tropical sun, the Yankees slowly rounded into shape, loosening their muscles in the heat, getting their eye on the ball again. After three weeks of delighting the local citizens and armed-forces installations in the area with their display of old-time power, the Yankees moved on to St. Petersburg for a short stay and several games.

As the team started North, the fans flocked to the ball parks to see the Yankees in action or, more properly, they came to see DiMaggio in action. Not since the days of Babe Ruth, the sportswriters noted, had one man so attracted the attention of the ordinary baseball fan. Not since Ruth had any one man in baseball so captured the imagination.

Curiously, too, DiMaggio seemed to be reacting differently now to the adulation of the fans. It had always embarrassed him, even annoyed him, and he wouldn't hesitate to show his annoyance with a curt remark or a cloak of silence. He had even been guilty of tactlessness at times, both with hero-worshiping fans and ballplayers. Frankly, he often preferred to be alone, and he alienated not a few people with his attitude.

The change may have been due to several things—his wartime service, his domestic troubles, and the maturity that came with being a father, or the simple knowledge of experience. But the change was there for those with sharp eyes to see, and one reporter went so far as to question Joe about his sudden "graciousness."

"I'll tell you," Joe said one day during a stopover for an exhibition game in Nashville. "It used to bother me a lot, the kids asking me for my autograph all the time, and the ones with the cameras, always wanting to take my picture. And especially those gushy ones, adults mostly, who always came up to me in hotel lobbies and restaurants and introduced themselves. I never felt comfortable with strangers, and frankly, I'd duck these people whenever I could, or brush them off.

"I can't say I like all that now, 'cause I don't. Most of the time I purposely grin because I'm tired of being called a sourpuss. I want people to like me, and I try to like them. I'm learning to take all that stuff, and I guess maybe, if I could relax and smile a little more, it would be better all around."

DiMaggio had come a long way from the shy, reticent kid who arrived in St. Petersburg ten years before. He had, as one sportswriter put it, "gained a personality." He was still aloof and moody, and there were periods of time when he did not talk to anyone for as long a period as a week. At other times, at least with people he knew well, he seemed at ease and more friendly.

Joe and the Yankees opened the 1946 season with a dash. They were in perfect shape, ready for a quick getaway, and they jumped right out in front. There was a new addition to the Yankee bench, too, to root them on. Almost daily Joe brought his four-year-old son to the ball park with him. The little fellow became a familiar sight in front of the Yankee dugout, playing catch with himself, the fielder's glove on his hand reaching to his elbow.

One day little Joe, as all the Yankees called him, was playing in front of the dugout, a catcher's mask covering his face. Joe McCarthy, coming up the dugout steps from the Yankee dressing room, looked at the youngster amusedly.

"Get that mask off him and stick a bat in his hand, Joe," the manager advised. "A DiMaggio doesn't look right unless he has a bat in his hands."

DiMaggio grinned affectionately at his son. A Yankee veteran, standing nearby, shook his head sagely. "Boy, does DiMag love that kid," he said to a dugout visitor. "Take a look at the expression on his face, willya? Look at his eyes. When it comes to little Joe, they can't call DiMag a dead pan!"

The Yankee bubble burst after the first six weeks of the season. DiMaggio, who had rapped twenty home runs in the first forty-one games, suddenly stopped hitting. And when DiMaggio stopped hitting, the Yankees stopped winning.

Joe was just about reaching a batting peak again when an injury sidelined him. This time he injured his leg sliding into second and was out for three weeks during the month of July.

When he finally did come back to the lineup, he

couldn't regain his batting touch. Everyone thought it was just temporary. This, after all, was DiMaggio. But something was missing. He was off somewhere. Opposing hurlers still found him to be no pushover, but he wasn't the same deadly man at the plate.

Then all of a sudden a new source of trouble hit DiMaggio a blow. As he took batting practice one day he felt a pain in the heel of his left foot, as if there were a nail in his shoe. He took off his shoe, examined it, ran his finger around the inside of the heel, but found nothing. Still the pain cut into every fiber of his foot, especially when he tried to run.

The Yankee trainer padded the shoe and backed the heel, but it didn't help. Playing became torture for Joe, but he stuck in there every day. Even with him in the lineup the Yankees were having their troubles. Without him, he knew without being vain about it, they would sink to the second division.

That the Yankees wound up in third place that year was due to Joe's insistence that he stay in the lineup despite his painful heel. For the first time in his career, he hit less than .300 for a season. He wound up with a .290 average, hitting 25 home runs and batting in 95 runs.

This was a record many major-league ballplayers would have been proud of, but DiMaggio could only think of it as a miserable failure.

The pain in his left heel by now was unbearable. The Yankees, worrying about it, too, sent him to have it thoroughly examined and X-rayed. The test showed a bone spur, a not uncommon condition with athletes and people whose occupation required them to be on their feet for long periods of time. With an athlete, however, the effects can be disastrous. Still, the doctors seemed optimistic. "An operation to remove the spur, and you'll be as good as new," they assured Joe.

18

The early-morning fog hugged the tall buildings in New York. It was still dark, but a group of shivering Yankee ballplayers converged on the mid-Manhattan hotel and waited in the wet coldness of the February dawn for the bus that was to take them to LaGuardia Airport.

George Stirnweiss, the Yankee second baseman, huddled deeper into his overcoat. "Man," he said to no one in particular, "I'll sure be glad to get down to Puerto Rico. Imagine, here we are, freezing our heads off, and tonight we'll be swimming down there."

"Yeah," Tommy Henrich pitched in, "we're really gonna see the world on this spring-training trip. Puerto Rico, Cuba, Venezuela. Whatever happened to the old-fashioned St. Petersburg camp?"

"That's after the tour," Stirnweiss came back. "First we have to bring culture to the tropics. Then it's on to St. Pete."

"What time's the plane taking off?" someone asked.

"Never, for all I care," shortstop Phil Rizzuto answered. "This flying business ain't for me. I don't mind touring, but I don't like planes."

"Well, fasten your safety belts," Henrich said. "Here comes the bus."

"Does the driver know we got to stop off and pick up DiMag?" Rizzuto asked, as the players clambered aboard.

"Sure—or anyway he'd better know," Henrich said. "What would we do without Joe?"

The bus rumbled through the silent streets and stopped at another midtown hotel. After a moment, DiMaggio came out of the lobby, limping slightly on his left foot. He wore a soft slipper over the bandage covering the heel section, which had been operated on in January. Forty stitches had been required to close the incision.

Joe gingerly eased his way into a seat, and the bus took off for the airport.

After a week in Puerto Rico, Dr. Mal Stevens, the Yankees' physician, took a good look at the wound. "It's healing nicely," he said to Joe, "but I think we can speed it along, if you like."

"Sure I want to speed it," Joe said. "I'd like to be able to play on Opening Day."

"Well, I wouldn't want to guarantee that, but I think plastic surgery will close the wound faster. I've been in touch with Dr. Bennett at Johns Hopkins, and he's ready to perform a skin graft whenever you want to go up there."

Joe nodded. "I'm ready now."

So it was back to Baltimore for Joe, where Dr. Bennett had performed the initial operation on the bone spur. In the second operation, Dr. Bennett took a skin graft from DiMaggio's thigh and planted it on the raw flesh surrounding the original incision. In March, Joe rejoined the

Yankees, this time in St. Petersburg. He went straight to the office of the new Yankee manager, Bucky Harris.

The skipper greeted him warmly. The two men knew each other only casually. "How're you feeling, Joe?" Harris asked.

"A little woozy, but ready to get back into shape," Joe said.

"Yeah, we'll take it easy at first, you know."

Joe nodded. "Dr. Bennett said no heavy work for three weeks yet, Bucky. Just loosening up."

The Yankee pilot glanced at the calendar. "I guess that means you won't be able to play for the first couple of weeks of the regular season, at least."

Joe grimaced. "It looks that way. But I'll be giving it my best."

"I know you will, Joe. I'm sure you know how much the boys and I are counting on you."

DiMaggio shook hands with the manager and left the office. Harris turned to one of his assistants. "If we can only stay close to the leaders until Joe's ready. If we can keep within four or five games of them by the time he's back and playing, we'll beat them all."

In New York, just before Opening Day, DiMaggio again talked to Bucky Harris. "I'm ready to start, Bucky," he told the startled pilot.

Harris thought for a minute. The temptation to put his star slugger into the Opening Day lineup was great, but . . .

"Joe, I think another week or so to kind of take things easy would be better for you before you break in."

"But I tell you I'm ready now," was Joe's comeback.

"Listen, Joe," Harris said. "I know how eager you are to

play, to help the team. And I appreciate it. But it won't help anybody if you break in too soon and maybe hurt yourself for the rest of the season. Another week, or at least a few more days, then we'll see what Dr. Stevens says. Okay?"

Joe seemed impatient. "Okay, you're the boss. A couple more days."

Before the season was a week old Joe climbed back into the lineup, wearing a high shoe on his left foot to protect the heel. The first time up at the plate Joe promptly celebrated his return with a three-run homer.

Despite the opening blast, however, it was quickly apparent that Joe had come back to play too soon. He was tired and was favoring his left foot. His hitting was way off, and by the middle of May it had fallen to below .250. To regain his batting eye, each day Joe took long hours of extra batting practice. As a result, he got into his first argument with the Yankee president, Larry MacPhail.

MacPhail, a promotion-minded executive, asked Joe and some other Yankees one day to pose for publicity pictures before game time.

Several of the Yankees refused, including Joe. "I can't spare the time from my batting practice," Joe said. "I'm worried about my hitting, not about your promotions."

MacPhail, enraged, fined several players, including DiMaggio and Charlie Keller, one hundred dollars each. The newspapers were up in arms against MacPhail, for his promotion stunts were becoming the butt of jokes in baseball circles. And to fine his players, especially men like Keller and DiMaggio, seemed high-handed indeed.

The fine, together with the humiliation that went with the publicity, left a permanent scar on DiMaggio. He never forgave MacPhail for it, though they publicly appeared to be friendly thereafter.

The indignation, however, perhaps served to jolt DiMaggio out of his batting doldrums. The night the news broke, the Yankees were playing the Detroit Tigers at the Stadium. By way of answer to MacPhail's fine, Joe won the game with a bases-loaded double off Hal Newhouser in the seventh inning.

The next day Joe got two hits, a single and a triple, and the next day two more. The Yankees started a western swing, and still Joe kept on hitting. In Cleveland the Yankees battled it out for second place with the Indians. With the score 7–7 in the eighth inning, Joe unloaded his second home run of the day, this time with the bases loaded, to sew up the ball game and put the Yankees ahead of their rivals.

But could life ever again flow smoothly for Joe? The next day, getting off a long throw to nip a runner at the plate, he felt a sharp pain in his elbow. He shook it off, for the elbow had been bothering him sporadically for several weeks. The next inning, he caught a fly ball in deep center field for the first out of the inning. He casually tossed the ball to the infield, but the ball bounced several feet in front of shortstop Rizzuto. No one noticed particularly, since it was assumed that Joe had just lobbed the ball in short. But in the field, Joe shook his arm a couple of times, then felt it gingerly. No doubt about it now, he thought.

After the game he went to see Manager Bucky Harris. "My arm is dead," he told the Yankee skipper simply.

Harris looked up at him. "Dead?" he repeated, unbelieving. "Are you sure?"

Joe nodded. "I can't throw a long ball without feeling like my arm's coming off."

Harris leaned his elbows on his desk and cupped his chin in his hands. "Great," he said. "What do we do now?"

"I suggest we don't do anything," Joe said. "I just wanted to let you know, that's all."

"You think you can still play with it?" Harris asked.

Joe nodded. "I can make the routine throws. I'll save my arm as much as possible. We'll let [Johnny] Lindell and Henrich in on it, so they can do some covering up for me. Otherwise, we'll keep this a secret."

Harris agreed wearily. "If this gets out they'll be running wild on the bases against you. It doesn't bother your hitting though?"

"No. Not a bit."

"Okay," Harris said. "What you can do is hold the ball in your hand after a catch and fake a throw. Do it in a pinch. Let's pray nobody tries to run. If they do, we're dead."

As the season progressed, rumors began making the rounds that DiMaggio's arm wasn't as strong as it used to be. But no one suspected how bad it really was. Base runners, from force of habit, played it safe on hits out to DiMaggio.

There were days now when he played in a fog of constant pain. The heel, not given a complete chance to rest, throbbed and burned from the irritation caused by his hard running. The arm felt like lead from shoulder to fingertips, and a glandular condition in the neck had developed to make his life completely miserable.

In August, the Red Sox came to New York. Joe was

exhausted, but he wouldn't stay out of the lineup. He sat one evening talking to Toots Shor in the latter's restaurant. Shor knew his friend's trouble and asked how things were going with him physically.

The Yankee Clipper, as Joe had begun to be called because of his graceful movements afield, shook his head sadly. "I can hardly lift the arm. One good throw a day, that's all I can get out of it. I try to save it, so I'll be able to throw a good one if something comes up during a game. That's the way it is, Toots."

The occasion came up right in that series with Boston. In one game, the Yankees were locked in an extra-inning, scoreless duel with the Red Sox. In the eleventh, with one out, Ted Williams stood perched on second with a double. The next batter singled to left-center. Williams tore around third and headed for the plate. The ball was hit so deep that no one expected DiMaggio to attempt the play.

But this was the time for that one good throw. Joe grabbed the ball on a hop and in one motion threw in to catcher Aaron Robinson. An uncontrollable cry of pain escaped Joe's lips and a wave of dizziness swept over him. He remained bent over after the follow-through, and never saw the play. But Robinson was waiting with Joe's perfect peg—and Williams was out!

Joe shook his head to clear the cobwebs and trotted back to his position. Sweat poured down his body from the pain and the dizziness. He took a deep breath and prayed the next batter wouldn't hit one out his way.

That's the way it went the rest of the season. Every day was like the day before, filled with pain and despair. Joe prayed that he wouldn't have to try to throw a runner out any more than once a game. But so complete was his deception, none tried to take liberties on the basepaths.

Even when the Yankees clinched the pennant, he refused to get out of the lineup. First, he feared his arm would stiffen up entirely if he rested. Second, he meant to carry his deception through the World Series. If he allowed himself to be benched now, the National Leaguers would suspect something was wrong with him.

The Dodgers were the National League champs that year and the World Series was a kind of inaugural game of the postwar era. New faces were on both teams, replacing the greats of the prewar days. For the Yankees, it was Snuffy Stirnweiss on second base and George McQuinn on first. A trio of catchers—Aaron Robinson, Sherman Lollar, and Yogi Berra—had replaced Bill Dickey.

The Dodgers had a raft of players on the roster who hadn't played against the Yankees in the 1941 series—Jackie Robinson, Eddie Stanky, Bruce Edwards, Spider Jorgensen, and practically the entire pitching staff.

Ralph Branca of the Dodgers started against Spec Shea in the Series opener, and the Dodger youngster had things all his own way until the fifth inning. Then DiMaggio opened with a single—and the riot was on. Five Yankee runs crossed the plate before the fire was put out. That was all the Bombers needed to win.

It looked like another Yankee *blitzkrieg* coming up when they won the second game, 10–3, but the Dodgers weren't dead yet. They came back to take the third game, 9–8, despite some scary moments. DiMaggio hit a home run and a single to drive in three Yankee runs, but Hugh Casey got him to rap into a double play in the eighth with the tying run on base.

The Series was tied the next day when the Dodgers beat Floyd Bevens in the ninth inning, 3–2. In beating the Yankee hurler, they also spoiled his no-hit game.

Ahead 2–1 in the final frame, with immortality in his grasp, Bevens walked two men, and pinch-hitter Cookie Lavagetto doubled off the right-field wall for the ball game—and the only hit off the losing hurler.

The Yankees came back to win the fifth game, 2–1, on DiMaggio's solo home run in the fifth inning. It was the Yankee Clipper's second home run of the Series. But the tenacious Dodgers sent the series into seven games, taking the next contest, 8–6. This game provided one of the Series highlights, at the expense of DiMaggio.

In the sixth inning, with the score 8–5, Brooklyn, the Yankees got two runners on base with a walk and a single. Joe, up next, swung from the heels and drove a long fly ball to left field. Everybody in Yankee Stadium figured it for the game-tying home run, including DiMaggio.

But little Al Gionfriddo, playing left field for Brooklyn, never gave up on it. Just in front of the 415-foot marker, at the Dodgers' bullpen, he turned and leaped upward, grabbing the ball just as it was about to drop in for a home run. It was one of the most remarkable catches in World Series history.

The final game was an anticlimax, for the Yankees won it easily, 5–2.

Right after the World Series, Larry MacPhail, the Yankees president, announced that he had sold his interest to his associates Dan Topping and Del Webb. But DiMaggio made the bigger news when he finally disclosed that he had been playing practically the entire season with a "dead" arm, and that it would be operated on over the winter.

In November, the baseball writers showed how much they had liked "that guy." For the third time in his career

Joe won the Most Valuable Player award, something no American League Player had ever done before. The Yankee Clipper hit .315 that year, not a great average. But the scribes knew that without Joe DiMaggio there would have been no Yankee pennant.

One of the most fantastic things about Joe's record that year was that he led the league in fielding percentage with .997. Despite the handicap of his injured heel and dead arm, DiMaggio made only a single error in the 141 games he played.

19

Joe DiMaggio sat in the dugout at Boston's Fenway Park and wondered about the last time he had spent a day free from racking pain. Since the war, he mused, he had not been without an ache or serious injury. Not that he'd been the picture of health before the war, he admitted to himself. He recalled offhand that he had failed to be around on Opening Day at least six seasons because of some ailment, and, as a matter of fact, he remembered that a sportswriter once told him that 1942 was the only year in which he had played a full 154 games.

Before the war there had been sprains and bruises, and that trick knee that almost ruined him back in San Francisco. Last year was torment when the dead arm and the bone spur on the left heel crippled him. Over the winter of 1947–48 the elbow had been opened and the chips removed, and the left heel, if not like new again, at least seemed to be mending well.

It was in spring training this year that the right heel started to bother him. He shrugged it off at first as a bruise. Even a fellow as unlucky as he seemed to be couldn't possibly develop two bones spurs in a lifetime.

Joe shook his head at the memory. There was the doc looking at the X rays again, then looking at Joe like he was a doomed man. "It's coming right out of your heel bone, Joe," the doc had said to him. "It's maybe only an eighth of an inch long. But it'll stab you to death if you try to play on it. There will be days when you won't be able to stand the pain."

But he had played on it, because the Yankees were in the middle of a pennant fight with Boston and Cleveland, and they needed him. Despite the heel, he was hitting well. There was that day in Philadelphia—Joe's brow furrowed as he tried to pin down the day—May something or other, he'd won both ends of a double-header for the Yankees with a pair of home runs and a couple of other hits.

Then there was May 23—that was a date he would always remember. He smiled with satisfaction at the thought. What a day—three straight homers against Cleveland!

But the pain in his heel! It almost drove him out of his mind. Every step on the field felt like someone driving an ice pick into his foot. Padding, cushions, nothing helped. For a while, he had tried walking on his toes. Whew! What a bonehead idea that was! Walking that way strained his leg muscles and he developed a muscle injury so severe his thighs had to be wrapped tightly in bandages to enable him to play.

He remembered, too, with a wry grin, the incident with Jimmy Cannon, a sports columnist for the New York *Journal-American* who lived at his hotel in Manhattan. Joe was walking down a flight of stairs, one night after dinner, when Cannon spotted him. Joe had to negotiate the stairs one at a time, like a child, putting both feet down gingerly on the same step before he could take another one. The columnist had looked at him in astonishment.

"My gosh, Joe!" the man had exclaimed. "Are you crazy playing when you have to walk like that!"

"Just don't write anything about this, at least till the season is over," he begged Cannon.

Well, two more days and the season would be over, anyway. Maybe then he could get off these aching feet and do something about that spur. Another operation, probably. He grimaced. Lately he'd been spending more time in the hospital than on the ball field.

He looked up from the dugout as a trim, bespectacled player in a Red Sox uniform walked into the batting cage to take his practice swings. The player looked over and waved to him. Joe grinned. Dom, his kid brother, the "Little Professor," as he was called, was the Red Sox center fielder. And a great one.

It was because of Dom that Joe was sitting in the dugout. Bucky Harris, the Yankee pilot, had asked DiMaggio if he wanted to stay out of the Red Sox series. It was the last two games of the season, and Bucky knew that Joe had been playing on sheer nerve since Opening Day.

The way the pennant picture shaped up, Boston needed both these games to tie Cleveland for the pennant, while the Yankees, if they won both the games, would still trail the Indians and could only tie Boston for second place. Since the pennant, therefore, was no longer at stake, Harris told Joe he might as well sit out these final two games, but Joe refused.

"Nothing doing, Bucky," he said. "I'm playing both games. Got to play."

"But Joe," the skipper protested, "enough's enough. Okay, while we were still fighting for the pennant I was glad to see you in there, even though I knew it was killing you, but we can't win anymore. Why ask for a couple extra days of torture?"

"I'll tell you why," Joe said. "My brother Dom's with the Red Sox. And nobody in Cleveland or anyplace else is gonna say I rolled over and played dead so my brother's team would have a better chance. I can't do that."

"Nobody'd accuse you of doing a thing like that," Harris assured him.

"Maybe not in public. But somebody, somewhere, would say it—or think it. I'm not giving anybody the chance to have that feeling. I've had enough said about me already. I've heard the boos."

Harris shrugged. "If that's the way you want it, Joe."

Now Joe sat there in the shade of the dugout and looked at Dom taking his swings. He had to confess he'd been wrong about Dom. When the Red Sox had first brought him up, by purchasing his contract from the San Francisco Seals in 1940, he never thought Dom could make it. Dom not only made the big leagues, but also Boston fans would give you an argument about Dom's superiority over Joe. Boston fans, as a matter of fact, had concocted a little parody to the tune of "Maryland, My Maryland" with which they serenaded Joe when he played Fenway Park. The song went:

> He's better than his brother Joe
> Do-mi-nic Di-Mag-gio

Well, now his kid brother was going to get married, too. Right after the season ended. And today and tomor-

row Mom and Pop and brother Tom would be in the
stands to watch Joe and Dom play against each other.
They all came in for the wedding and were sitting in a
box behind the Boston dugout now. From where he sat
Joe could see his mom, the same as ever, and Pop a lot
grayer than he remembered him, but looking very spry.

A baseball writer was talking to Pop. "Are you rooting
for either of your sons, Mr. DiMaggio? Or are you neu-
tral?"

One of Joe's sisters translated the question into Italian,
for Mr. DiMaggio's English was still limited.

Mr. DiMaggio nodded toward the man in the batting
cage. "I hope Dominic win this time," he said. "Giuseppe,
he win all the time."

Well, Giuseppe, pain or no pain, family or no family,
outdid himself trying to win again. He got three hits that
day, including a homer, but the Sox won anyway.

Then it was the last day of the season, and if Boston
won they'd be tied for first with Cleveland, and there'd be
a playoff for the pennant. In the stands, no one rooted
harder for the Red Sox to win than Papa DiMaggio.

In the second inning Joe singled, and Papa DiMaggio
fidgeted in his seat. In the fifth, with Boston ahead by
two runs, Joe doubled, driving in a run, and Papa DiMaggio muttered under his breath.

The Red Sox had a three-run lead now, in the seventh.
But Joe smacked a drive off the wall and hobbled into
second with a double. In his box seat down the third-base
line, Papa DiMaggio turned angrily to his family.
"What'sa matter with Giuseppe! Why all the time he hit
the ball so good?"

By the time the ninth inning rolled around, Joe just

managed to drag his aching body into the batter's box. He deliberately let the first two pitches go by, though one was a beauty, because he needed the moment's rest after walking from the dugout. When the pain had subsided enough for him to get his bearings, he picked out a fast ball and drove it against the left-field wall, his fourth straight hit of the afternoon. Joe limped into first and held on.

Pains like hot irons shot through his body as he stood on first base after running out the hit. In the dugout, Bucky Harris called time and sent a pinch runner in for Joe. The Yankees were behind now by five runs, and Harris figured Joe might as well call it a season right here.

As Joe limped off the field, the crowd at Fenway Park stood up and gave him one of the greatest ovations of his life. Joe touched the peak of his cap in acknowledgment. For the moment he forgot the pain, feeling happier than he'd been in a long time.

That Joe was able to play out the 1948 season in his condition, missing only one game, was amazing enough. But the way he played it was strictly storybook stuff. He batted .320 and led the league in home runs with 39, and in runs batted in with 155.

In November Dr. Bennett of Johns Hopkins operated on Joe's right heel to remove the bone spur. Three weeks later a reporter visited Joe at his hotel in New York. The Clipper was sitting in an easy chair, relaxing in a dressing gown and reading a book. On the table next to the chair was a framed photograph of Joe and little Joe, both in Yankee uniform.

"How's the foot, Joe?" the reporter asked.

DiMaggio looked down at the bandaged member.

"Coming along all right," he said. "I'll be able to walk on it with crutches in about a week. After that I'll switch to a cane for a while. When I'll be able to get a shoe on it, though, I don't know."

"You think you'll be okay by spring training?"

"I'm pretty sure I will. Dr. Bennett says this wound will heal faster than the one I had on my left foot because he went in at a different place. You know, I get all sorts of letters from people who have the same trouble. Doormen and mailmen and people like that who stand on their feet a lot. They all want to know whether an operation helps."

"What do you tell them?"

"Well," Joe said, "it looks like it helped me."

But Joe was wrong. He didn't know it then, of course, but he was terribly wrong.

For six weeks Joe hobbled around his hotel room contentedly. When he pressed down on his right foot he didn't feel a single twinge. He marched around with a cane, dropping in to Toots Shor's for lunch now and then with his good friend George Solotaire, the Broadway ticket broker. In February Joe limped over to the Yankee business office and signed the best contract of his career, calling for a salary of about ninety thousand dollars. It was ample evidence of the Yankees' faith in his ability to play the entire season.

But later that month the pain started to come back. Joe began worrying again. Spring training was only two weeks away. He decided to stick it out and see what happened down South.

He said nothing to Casey Stengel, the new Yankee manager, when he reported to St. Petersburg. But after the first day's workout he knew it was no use ignoring it. The heel hurt as badly as it did before the operation.

Stengel had no choice other than to send Joe back to Johns Hopkins Hospital for an examination. There, Dr. Bennett diagnosed the condition as a "thickening in the heel" that should disappear in a short while with ordinary precautions.

When Joe got back to St. Petersburg, Stengel called him into his office.

"Joe," he said, "nobody can tell how that thing hurts you, including me. So I'm not gonna tell you how and when to train. You work out the way you feel. I know you're gonna do your best for the club, no matter what."

"Thanks, Case," Joe returned. "I'm not worried about my fielding too much. I think I'll just try to take as much batting practice as possible to keep my eye. How I'll keep my legs in shape, I don't know."

Every day, before and after his light workout, Joe went through the routine of whirlpool baths and heat treatments. He wore sponge-rubber cushions in his shoes, finally removing the spikes from the heel of his right baseball shoe. But his heel was still so painful he could hardly walk, much less run.

The exhibition season was a nightmare for DiMaggio. At first, he asked Stengel to give him pinch-hitting roles. He found he couldn't even dig in at the plate without biting his lips to keep from crying out. On March 30, however, he asked Stengel to start him, and he stuck it out for four games.

In a game in Beaumont, Texas, he had to leave in the seventh inning, limping off the field. But he tried again the next day in Greenville. Again he had to leave the game, sweating with pain. The next stop was Dallas, and the field was soft from an early-morning rain.

"If I'm ever going to snap out of it, this is the place,"

Joe said to a teammate. "If I can't play in this mud—" he shook his head.

After two innings he asked Manager Stengel to take him out. It was no use. He couldn't hit and he couldn't field. He played 43 innings of exhibition baseball, had gotten 7 hits, none of them home runs, in 31 at-bats for a .226 average.

It meant back to Baltimore and Johns Hopkins for more treatment. At the airport, a grim-visaged DiMaggio talked to reporters. "All I know is I'm going to miss the opening of a season again," he said resignedly. "I don't know when I'll be back. Whenever the doctors say it's all right." Then he walked out to the waiting plane, a dejected-looking figure, limping badly, shoulders stooped.

It was a bad day for flying. Storms covered the South, and the plane had to make frequent long stops because of the rain and the fog. Joe became airsick and he was a terrible sight when the first stop was made. Newspapermen gathered around him in the coffee shop. He was pale, nauseous, and tired, his heel stabbing at every step. He looked in the mirror behind the counter and was shocked at the reflection. His eyes were hollow, and dark circles stood out in a face that was chalk white. He needed a haircut, too.

The reporters plied him with questions.

"How's the heel?"

"What do the doctors say?"

"How long you going to be out?"

"Can it be cured?"

"Joe, are you going to quit baseball?"

Joe answered them all wearily. The heel hurt. He didn't

know how long he'd be out or what the chances for complete recovery were.

In every city where the plane stopped the routine was repeated. The same questions, always the same questions. He was getting angry—especially when they asked about his quitting baseball. It was something that had been occupying his mind ever since the heel started hurting again. He hated being reminded of it. He hated the questions hammered at him over and over. He hated the nosy reporters. He hated everything.

It was a relief to reach the hospital. Here at least he'd have peace, he thought. He should have known better. They were wheeling him up to the operating room, his arms and legs strapped to the table, a white sheet covering him except for his head. Suddenly there was a flash of light. A photographer had snapped his picture.

Joe screamed at the man. "What's wrong with you? Do you have to do that now? What'll my folks think if they see a picture of me like this in the papers?"

The photographer hesitated. Joe calmed his voice down. "Look," he said, "I've always played ball with you guys. Come up to my room later and take all the pictures you want. But don't print that one."

The photographer looked at Joe a long moment. Then he said, "Okay, Joe. I'll tear up the negative. I'm just trying to do my job, you know."

"I know," DiMaggio said. "I appreciate it."

For the next couple of days Joe tried to get some rest. There was a "Do Not Disturb" sign on his hospital door but all day and half the night he could hear the noises outside. People opening his door, walking in to see him—

reporters, autograph hunters, well-wishers, cranks with sure cures and people who were just morbidly curious.

He tried to keep the date of his discharge from the hospital a secret. He wanted more than anything else to get away to New York quietly. But on April 14, as he hobbled slowly through the hospital lobby on a pair of crutches, he was intercepted by photographers and reporters. The flashbulbs popped and the questions were hurled at him. Suddenly something snapped in him.

"Leave me alone, all of you!" he shouted. "Don't you think you've gone far enough? You're driving me batty! Now, get the blazes away from me."

A reporter answered him calmly. "The fans are interested in you, Joe."

"Well I got to think of myself, too," Joe shouted. "This is darn tough on me. Don't you think all this is affecting me? Now, leave me alone!"

Back in his hotel room in New York, Joe brooded silently. He would see no one, talk to no one on the telephone except his two friends Toots Shor and Jimmy Ceres. Joe sat hour after hour, day after day, in the darkened room, looking at nothing, seeing nothing. The doctors at Johns Hopkins had told him little to make him optimistic. His heel trouble was "an immature calcium deposit" whatever that meant. How long would he be out of action? All they could tell him was, "The length of the disability will be determined by the results of the treatment."

Thanks for nothing, Joe thought. They mean they don't know and I may be crippled like this forever and never play ball again.

Back in New York he sank back into despair. At first he tried to go out during the day to get some air, to clear his head. He stopped in at Shor's, but friends and strangers alike came over and sympathized. It embarrassed Joe and it annoyed him. Why couldn't they understand that he wanted to be left alone?

Sometimes, late at night, he tried to slip unnoticed into a movie, to ease his mind for a few hours. But he was always recognized, and the people around him came over with all sorts of pads and pieces of scrap paper for his autograph. He gave up going to the movies.

Most of the time he sat in his room alone with his gloomy thoughts. Sometimes he watched the ball games on television. Maybe he could keep his batting eye that way. But from the angle of the TV cameras he couldn't judge a pitch. When he found himself shouting out loud about the plate umpire's ball-and-strike calls, he knew it was time to call an end to television baseball.

When they could get away from their businesses, Shor and Ceres dropped in to keep him company. In their work, they had become practiced listeners, and both Shor and Ceres could sit and listen to Joe rave on indefinitely, nodding their heads in apparent agreement.

"What am I knocking myself out for, anyway?" Joe ranted one evening. "Who needs baseball? What do I have to show for it? I'll tell you what I got to show for it! Look! Scars on my right arm from the elbow operation. Scars on my heels. Swollen feet and two big charley horses. And ulcers! That's what I got from baseball!" He paced back and forth like a caged animal, muttering to himself, while his two friends calmly continued their game of gin rummy.

Mostly, though, Joe sat by himself in the darkened room. Outside, he could see the bright lights of Broad-

way, and the noises of the traffic came up to him with the
warm breeze that floated in through the open window
and fluttered the filmy curtains.

These nights were the worst. One sentence repeated itself over and over in his mind: I'm all through, all
through with my baseball life. Through—all through. Am
I through? *Am I through?* It pounded in his ears till he
had to get out of his chair to turn up the radio vol-
ume in order to drown out the sound of that tormenting
thought.

The nights were filled with sleeplessness. He lay awake
staring at the ceiling, watching the reflection of the
flickering hotel sign. Click-click, click-click, click-click, it
went. Then, suddenly, when he couldn't make out the
reflection against the whiteness of the ceiling he realized
it was dawn.

What could he do? What could he do? What if his career should be over, what could he do? He paced the
floor, limping on his crippled foot, smoking cigarette after
cigarette. He tried to read a magazine, but quit after the
first sentence. He looked at the newspapers. He turned to
the sports section. Finding the Yankees had lost, he threw
the paper on the floor in disgust.

"It can't be all over!" he shouted in anguish one night.
He went to the closet and flung open the door. He looked
at his custom-tailored suits hanging neatly on the rack,
the expensive shoes lined up on the floor. He slammed the
door shut and stalked around the room, stopping at the
picture of himself and little Joe on the table. What about
all the plans he had for him? College, Harvard maybe.
Unlike his father, he would have an education. He

wouldn't be ashamed to mix with people—all kinds of people—for fear he'd appear ignorant.

What about all the things he'd planned to do for his mother and his brothers and sisters? Baseball has been good to me, Joe prayed silently; let it be good to me just a little bit more. What else do I know how to do? And how else can I do all the things I've yet to do?

Three thousand miles away, in the privacy of her bedroom, Rosalie DiMaggio was praying, too, as she did every night and every morning. First, she prayed for her departed Giuseppe, a good man. Then she prayed for all her children. And then she added a special prayer for her Joe—that he should get well and be happy again.

Joe awoke one morning feeling fine. For a change, he had had a good night's sleep. He got out of bed carefully, easing his injured foot onto the floor. He put a little weight on the foot, then he looked down at it. Wasn't it touching the floor? He didn't feel any pain. He pressed down harder. Still no pain. He felt the heel with his hand. It was usually hot and feverish. Now it felt cool.

He couldn't believe it. He was afraid to believe it. Afraid it was just a temporary thing. He walked around the room, and around and around again, waiting for the pain to come back. But it didn't come back. He dressed carefully and walked out into the street. The sidewalk felt hard under his feet, still there was no pain. He walked around the streets of Manhattan and he didn't mind a bit when people stopped him and asked how he felt and when several of them asked for his autograph.

He went around to Toots Shor's for lunch. "Hey, Fat

Guy"—Joe beckoned to Shor—"You know what? The foot feels so good today, I think I'm gonna start playing after a couple of days of practice."

It was hard to keep from grinning and bursting out with the news to everybody, but he didn't want to be premature, in case the pain should return. Besides, the Yankees were out of town. If the heel still felt this good when they came back, he was going to give them a walloping surprise!

On June 14 the Yankees returned. When Joe walked into the clubhouse that morning he was greeted with nods or short hellos by the players and the sportswriters. By now they all knew how Joe felt—no questions, no talk about the foot.

Joe walked over to his locker and got into his uniform. Everyone looked at him curiously, wondering. It was the first time he had bothered to suit up that year. Joe just dressed quietly and went out onto the playing field, trailed by the writers. The players dressed quickly and followed them out.

Joe just stood around a while, drinking in the sunshine and the smell of the Yankee Stadium grass, while the rest of the players went about their practice. The sportswriters were dying to ask Joe why he was in uniform, but they restrained themselves.

Then, after a while, Joe picked up a bat and walked over to the batting cage. Everyone stopped to watch him. He stepped into the batter's box carefully at first. Slowly, testing his heel, he set himself, dug his spikes into the dirt. It felt okay. He took batting practice till his hands were blistered from gripping the bat. His batting eye was way off, but that was nothing. The important thing was that he could put his full weight on his right foot without any pain. Although the players and the writers noticed this, still no one tried to question him.

The next day Joe took batting practice again, and spent a few minutes fielding ground balls in the infield and chasing a couple of pop flies. Early the next morning he had one of the batting-practice catchers hit fungos to him in the outfield for half an hour, and he ran around the field a couple of times. When the workout was over he was dead tired. The heel was a little sore, but it was still cool and the ache soon subsided.

Joe worked out for a week, and though the writers with the club refrained from questioning him, they speculated on his return. Most of them figured another three weeks to a month before Joe would be in good enough shape to play again—that is, if his heel was really all right. They didn't know—and Joe wasn't ready to offer the information.

There was a night exhibition game with the Giants coming up the next day, then a series in Boston. The Red Sox, winning ten out of their last eleven games, were breathing down the necks of the league-leading Yankees. Joe thought it was high time he started earning his ninety thousand dollars.

He went to see Stengel. "Case," he told the manager, "I'd like to start in the game with the Giants."

Stengel was startled. "You only been working out a week. Ain't you trying to get back a little too quick?"

"I'm okay, Case," Joe assured the manager. "Let me start."

"Sure, Joe," Casey agreed. "You just let me know when you've had enough."

The Yankee Clipper looked terrible that night, but the fans cheered his return wildly. Many of them had never expected to see Joe play a game again. Kirby Higbe, a knuckle-ball artist, pitched for the Giants, and Joe, away from real competition since the previous September, could only send four weak pop-ups to the infield. The heel held up fine throughout the exhibition game, however, and he didn't feel too tired. That was what he had intended to find out.

After the game, Joe said to Stengel, "I might be ready for the series with Boston. The heel held up pretty good." Casey nodded. "You're the boss," he said.

But the morning the team left for Boston, Joe stayed behind. He had to pick up a special shoe that afternoon, and he still wasn't sure whether he could play. Maybe it was too soon, he thought. Maybe I don't have the touch anymore and I'll lose the games for us. The team seems to be doing okay without me.

He had an afternoon snack with Toots Shor. The two men ate silently. Then Shor said, "Night game tonight, eh? Who's going for the Sox?"

"McDermott," Joe said. "Tough boy under the lights."

Shor looked at Joe, and Joe looked back at Shor. Suddenly Joe made up his mind. He dashed out of the restaurant and hailed a passing cab. "LaGuardia Airport," he instructed the driver. "And fast!"

20

Fenway Park was booming with sound. The loudspeaker calling out the lineups had just announced that Joe DiMaggio would play center field! The stands buzzed with excitement and expectancy. It was in this same park that Joe had last played a regular game, at the close of the 1948 season, and these same fans had given him an ovation as he hobbled off the field on his crippled legs. Now Joltin' Joe was back. But was he the Joe DiMaggio of old? The air was tense with anticipation.

Mickey McDermott sent the Yankees down in order in the first frame, and Allie Reynolds put down the Red Sox in their half. Joe came up to bat to lead off the Yankee half of the second. The crowd gave him a big hand, then waited expectantly. McDermott wound up, pitched—and Joe cracked the ball on a line over the shortstop's head for a single. The crowd roared, and Joe's teammates on the bench yelled to him happily. McDermott fanned Berra and Billy Johnson, but Johnny Lindell walked and Hank Bauer homered, and the Yankees were in front, 3–0.

In the next inning, with Rizzuto on first and two out, Joe came to bat again. This time he timed McDermott's

first pitch and blasted it high and deep to left field. Ted
Williams turned, ran two steps, and then watched as the
ball banged into the screen above the high left-field wall
for a home run!

Joe couldn't stop grinning as he trotted around the
bases. Rizzuto, Henrich, and the rest of the Yankee team
were waiting at home plate to slap him on the back. "Nice
goin', Joe!" "Great hitting, Joe!" they said to him. It was
just like old times.

In the fifth inning, Joe grounded to the pitcher. In the
eighth, he walked. Berra, next up, grounded to Bobby
Doerr at second base. Doerr flipped to shortstop Vern
Stephens to start the double play, but Joe came sliding
into the bag so hard he knocked the shortstop off his feet,
breaking up the double play. In the dugout, though,
Casey Stengel's heart was in his mouth. He watched to
see if DiMaggio could get up and walk away from that
slamming slide into second base. And until Joe had
picked himself up, dusted himself off, and trotted back to
the bench, the Yankee manager didn't dare breathe.

In the ninth inning the Red Sox knocked Reynolds
from the box, although the Yankees were leading, 5–4.
With Joe Page pitching in relief, there were two out, a
man was at third, and Ted Williams was up. The Boston
slugger picked out one of Page's serves and blasted it far
out to center field. DiMaggio turned, sailed out like the
Yankee Clipper of old, and caught the four-hundred-foot
drive like it was a pop fly. That was the ball game,
wrapped up neatly by Joe DiMaggio.

It was as fantastic a comeback game as could be concocted by a writer of fiction, and the sportswriters
dragged out all the superlatives in describing Joe's play

that night. "He played as if he'd never even been away or
sick a day in his life," one said. "It is beyond comprehen-
sion."

The sportswriters should have saved some of their ad-
jectives, however, for Joe was just getting warmed up.
The next day, still in Boston, the Yankees were behind,
7–1, when the Clipper came up with two out and two
men on. Joe leveled his war club and smacked another
home run, to make the score 7–4.

With DiMaggio coming back like this, could his mates
do any less? They rallied and tied the score, 7–7. Then
Joe came up again, and this time he cleared the screen
over the left-field wall with a tremendous home run to
win the ball game. As he trotted around third and came to
the plate, Joe was greeted in front of the dugout by Casey
Stengel, who bowed his head and held his hands out in
front of him.

In the third game with the Red Sox with two men on,
Joe rocketed another game-winning home run, his fourth
homer in three days! It was just too much for the
sportswriters to handle. What could they say? What
could anyone say? Everyone could only agree that it was
undoubtedly the most remarkable comeback in the history of baseball.

Once back in the lineup, Joe didn't let up for a minute.
He banged away at the opposition pitching in his same
old style, and covered the center-field pasture with his
usual assured grace. In the All-Star game he hit a double
and single, to drive in three runs. Through July and August he kept the Yankees up on top. Then, in September,
he was clipped again with hard luck. This time it was
virus pneumonia, and while the Yankee Clipper fretted in

bed the Red Sox caught the Yankees and finally passed them.

The Red Sox held a one-game lead over the Yankees as they came into the Stadium for the final two games of the season. All they needed was an equal break in the two games, and the pennant would go to Boston.

But the Saturday they came to town was "Joe DiMaggio Day." The citizens of New York were going to honor Joe with speeches and presents before the game. This was a day Joe didn't intend to miss.

Joe stood up at home plate and listened quietly as local dignitaries paid him homage. He was pale and gaunt from his siege with the pneumonia bug, but he was happy. And he was sad, too. His brother Dom was on hand, his little boy Joe, Jr., his mom, and his brother Tom. But Mom, Joe knew, wouldn't be with him much longer. She was suffering from cancer. He was glad she was still strong enough to make the trip East and see all this.

After the speeches there were gifts. A TV set, watches and jewelry, a speedboat, two automobiles, and dozens of other gifts. Finally Joe went to the microphone to make his speech. It was a short one.

"I just want to thank the Good Lord for making me a Yankee," he said simply. And he turned swiftly to hide the tears he could no longer hold back.

Then the game started—and Joe was a Yankee again. Fifteen pounds underweight, with a temperature of 102° and just up from a sickbed, but he stood up there with his bat in his hands and the pennant at stake and played the game the only way he knew how.

The first time he swung his bat, in the first inning, he

realized he was too weak to hit with any power. So for the first time in his life he shortened up on the bat and became a place hitter. The next two trips up he dropped a couple of singles into right field, and the Yankees won the game, 5–4. The pennant race was now tied.

The next day, still plunking hits into right field, Joe led the Yankees to the second victory over the Red Sox, 5–3, clinching the pennant!

There was still a World Series to be won, however, before the year could be closed out successfully. DiMaggio, who had hit .346 in the seventy-six games he played in his comeback trail, was tired and still sick. But somehow, he felt, the rest of the team worked together better when he played. He had read in the papers that one of them had said, "When the old Clipper is out there in center field, it gives a kind of lift. We know everything's going to be all right when Joe's in the lineup. We're lost without him."

So DiMaggio dragged his weary frame into the fray with the Brooklyn Dodgers. On the momentum of their final drive against the Red Sox, the Yankees took the Dodgers in five games. Playing when he should have been in bed, DiMaggio went into the final game of the Series with just a scratch single to his credit. But when he hit a home run into the upper deck of Ebbets Field in that last game, the fans stood up and gave him a rousing ovation. It was a fitting close to the most remarkable season in Joe's great career.

21

In the rapidly darkening twilight of his career, Joe Di-
Maggio made a brief reappearance as the healthy, vigor-
ous DiMaggio of old, like the final rally of a dying man.
He reported in the spring of 1950 tanned, robust, and fit,
and with a contract for one hundred thousand dollars.
But the sands were running out. Throughout the training
season he had only the minor complaints any baseball
player might come up with getting into shape—blisters on
his foot, a strained shoulder muscle, vague aches and
pains.

He felt better, physically and mentally, than he had
since before the war. He had been getting big money now
for three years, and his financial affairs were in good
shape. His heels weren't bothering him at all, which put
him at ease. He was hitting the ball with all the old
power in the exhibition games. He was, apparently, completely over the physical miseries of the 1949 season, and
was looking forward to a good year.

For the first three weeks of the season, Joe was making
his spring predictions about that good year look accurate.
Then he went into a rapid tailspin. On May 6 he fell

below .300. Soon he was down to .275. Then he hit .250 and was still going down. On June 17, he reached one of the lowest ebbs of his career. He was hitting .239, hardly a respectable average for a hundred-thousand-dollar-a-year man.

The epitaphs began to appear in the newspapers. To even the strongest DiMaggio adherent among the sportswriting fraternity, it appeared that Joe was through. Even Joe himself began to believe that this was more than just a normal slump. And one day Manager Casey Stengel called him into his office.

"How you feeling, Joe?" the cagey skipper asked.

DiMaggio hesitated a moment. "Not too hot, to tell you the truth, Case," Joe replied. "Nothing's bothering me in particular. But I just don't feel in top shape." He smiled sourly. "I guess I'm just getting old."

"You want to come out and take a rest for a while?"

"No"—Joe didn't hesitate—"I'm not going to start that kind of thing now. When I can't play every day I'll call it quits."

"Well," Stengel said, "I don't guess you're ready for that yet."

Joe shook his head. "I think I've got one, two more years yet. I want to help win the pennant—and if I can, next year's pennant. I still got enough left to do that."

With grim determination, Joe went out the next day and fought his way up the ladder. In a night game in Cleveland on June 20, he rapped two hits, the second one calling for a ceremony. It was the two-thousandth hit of Joe's career. He became the eighty-eighth man to hit that many in the history of baseball, and when Larry Doby fielded the ball and threw it back, the grass-stained horsehide was formally presented to Joe as a memento of the occasion.

There weren't too many more moments for mementos that summer. In the heat of August, after pulling his average up to a fairly respectable .270, Joe wilted. It was plain that the strain of playing every day was too much for him. In a stretch of eight games Joe got only four hits in thirty-eight times at bat.

On August 11, before the scheduled night game with the Philadelphia Athletics, Manager Stengel again called Joe in. This time there was no questioning on Stengel's part.

"Joe," he said right out, "I think you could use a little rest. You're looking peaked these days."

"I'll pull out of it, Case," Joe said.

But Stengel shook his head. "This is a tough pennant race, Joe. Right now's the time for us to take a deep breath and get set for a fight down to the finish. You take a few days off right here, when the heat's off a little, and you'll be okay when we need you at the windup."

DiMaggio looked at the manager. "Are you asking me or telling me, Case?"

Stengel scratched his head. "Well, I guess you'd have to say I was telling you."

That night, for the first time in his long career, Joe was benched for a reason other than a specific injury or illness. It attracted a substantial amount of comment, but was not wholly unexpected. In fact, many fans speculated that Stengel would have taken DiMaggio out sooner had Joe indicated a willingness to be relieved.

However Joe or anybody else might have felt about his being benched, everyone had to admit later that the results of his week's rest were spectacular. It seemed just the tonic he needed.

On August 18 Joe came back to play in a night game against the Athletics, and promptly won the game with a three-run home run. The next day he contributed a double and two singles as the Yankees won again, and Joe was off on a tear. Just as in so many previous years, as soon as the Clipper started banging the ball again, the rest of the Yankees joined the parade.

From third place when Joe came back to work, the Yankees zoomed to first by the middle of September, and won the pennant by three games over the Detroit Tigers. Since August 18 Joe had collected 55 hits for 140 times at bat, a .393 average. Included in his hits were 11 homers, 10 doubles, and 3 triples. He also batted in 41 runs during that brief span. And he wound up the season with a .301 average, just making the charmed circle with his final drive.

The Philadelphia Phillies' Whiz Kids, winners in the National League, were defeated in four straight games by the Yanks. The closest they came to a win was the second game, which went into extra innings a 1–1 tie. But since the Yankee Clipper was getting too old to play extra inning games, he broke it up in the tenth with a home run, for a 2–1 Yankee victory.

In the fourth game, just to show the Philadelphia youngsters that the stories about him were not fables, Joe knocked the Phils' starting hurler to the showers with a two-run double in the first inning, and the Whiz Kids went down without a murmur.

It was DiMaggio's ninth World Series and his eighth winning one. He hit a respectable .308 this time, and a couple of sportswriters speculated that Joe might retire, having wound up on a good note.

"Not yet," Joe said to this. "I've got an ambition. I want to play in ten World Series. I think I can carry my own weight into the next one, too. After that, well, I'll have to see."

But in the Yankees' new training camp at Phoenix, Arizona, the following spring, Joe was a lot more definite about his plans. "This will probably be my last year," he told reporters.

The Yankee camp was stunned at the announcement. Coaches Bill Dickey and Frankie Crosetti, who had played many years with Joe, and had been around when Babe Ruth and Lou Gehrig bowed out, agreed that Joe's retirement would mean the end of another baseball era.

Jerry Coleman, a young infielder, shook his head at the report. "All my life DiMaggio and the Yankees have been one and the same to me," he said. Phil Rizzuto agreed and added, "I'd sure hate to turn around and not see the big guy out there behind me."

But in the exhibition games it was apparent that the thirty-six-year-old DiMaggio didn't quite have it anymore. The spring was gone from his legs, the zip from his bat. He was playing from memory, doing a better job than many at their best, perhaps, but playing from memory nonetheless, like a battered pug who'd had one fight too many.

From the opening bell of the 1951 season Joe had nothing but troubles. He wasn't getting his base hits, and he wasn't feeling up to par physically. Playing became an effort for him, rather than a joy.

When Joe's mother died, in June, he became melancholy again. He avoided talking to his teammates as much as possible, and the sportswriters found him almost impossible to interview.

"Joe is like he was when he first broke in back in 1936," one writer said. "Only then it was shyness. Now Joe's just down in the dumps and feeling morose. The only trouble is, some of the Clipper's teammates are beginning to resent his attitude."

DiMaggio didn't realize it at first, but he was brewing a storm. It came to a head in July when Stengel pulled him suddenly out of a game in the second inning and benched him. The Yankee manager said he'd lifted Joe because one of the players said he saw Joe limping. But the official statement later from the club said that Joe was being rested, and mentioned no injury. Furthermore, a writer reported that DiMaggio and Stengel had exchanged sharp words in the clubhouse after the game.

The following day Joe was back in the lineup, but sliding into second to break up a double play, he pulled a muscle in his side and had to come out again. Then he and Stengel decided to straighten out a few things in public. They each had a long explanation to offer.

"I've never had any difference of opinion with Casey Stengel," Joe said. "And I've always enjoyed cordial relations with my Yankee teammates. I've given my best at all times and have never complained when Casey thought it wise to take me out of the lineup.

"I'm ready to do what I can," Joe continued. "If Casey wants me to pinch-hit for a while, I'll give it all I got."

The Yankee manager, for his part, was equally firm in his denial of a rift between himself and DiMaggio. "If I didn't like the feller, would I have picked him for the

All-Star team?" Stengel asked rhetorically. "He's been a great star for years and a great credit to baseball and the Yankees. Why should I have anything against him?"

"That thing up in Boston," he went on, "well, that was a lot made out of nothing by one of the Boston writers. He came into the dressing room when he shouldn't have, after I took out DiMaggio, and he caught Joe in a heated moment. Later the whole thing was straightened out, but naturally the feller wasn't around then."

Whatever the reasons, with each passing day Joe became more sullen, more silent, harder to live with. "I haven't seen Joe so glum since 1949," a friend of his remarked. "He hasn't even said hello to me the last few times he's seen me. He looks right through me—like I'm not even there."

Most of the sportswriters, at least those who had traveled with the Yankees for a number of years, explained away Joe's surliness with tolerance. Because of his overwhelming pride, and because he was a perfectionist, they said, he was lashed with inner torments when he failed to play up to the standards he had set for himself. He was unhappy and brooded over his inability to overcome his waning talent.

Some of the writers, however—and these were in the minority, and usually those who hadn't known Joe too well—merely put Joe's irascibility down to a sour disposition brought on by his fading career.

Everybody, however, forgot about Joe's disposition when his hitting started picking up again in August. He cracked out seven hits in fourteen times at bat during one stretch, and won three games in a row with timely hits. And when he injured his leg again, the Yankees began to worry about his availability for the coming stretch drive for the pennant.

Going into September it was still a four-way battle for the pennant. The Indians, the Red Sox, and the Tigers were all hustling along with the Yankees to win the coveted flag. Joe staggered back into the lineup after a couple of days and did his best. But all his old injuries, apparently, had come back together to go out in the same blaze of glory as the great man they had tormented for the thirteen years of his major-league life. The Yankee Clipper, battered but still going, staggered home with his teammates to another pennant, his tenth in thirteen seasons. His final average for the season was .263, the poorest in his career. He batted in 71 runs and hit 12 home runs, a record more than one major-league regular that year couldn't surpass. But for Joe, it was the handwriting on the wall—in capital letters. All that remained now was the realization of the ambition he had expressed at the end of the 1950 season, his tenth World Series.

After the first three games of the Series had gone into the books, however, Joe kind of wished he'd quit at nine World Classics. He hadn't hit in eleven times at bat, and the Giants were leading, two games to one. But Casey Stengel wasn't giving up on Joe yet.

"I gotta string along with the big guy," the Yankee manager said when a reporter asked him about the possibility of benching DiMaggio. "I gotta keep him batting in the cleanup spot, because he's been the heart of the ball club for so long. And because he's—well, because he's still DiMaggio. If he gets going, we'll beat the Giants. If he doesn't, we'll go down fighting."

Rain postponed the fourth game, and Joe took the time

off to ask advice of an old buddy of his, Lefty O'Doul, who had managed him one year in San Francisco. "You're swinging wrong," O'Doul advised. "You've been pressing, swinging at bad balls. Cut down on your swing. Relax, Joe. Just remember, don't press so much."

The first time at bat in the fourth game, however, Joe went down again. But the next time he singled, his first hit of the Series. And in the fifth inning he slammed a home run with Yogi Berra aboard to put that game on ice for the Yankees. Yogi, on second at the time, leaped in the air as Joe's drive dropped into the left-field seats. The spirit of the entire Yankee team seemed to take heart with that blow. They drove on to win the game, 6–2.

The next day Joe slammed a double and two singles as the Yankees routed five Giant hurlers in a 13–1 triumph. In the final game, which the Yankees took, 4–3, to win the World Championship, Joe walked twice, grounded out, and in the eighth inning doubled. As it turned out, that was his parting shot to baseball, and perhaps sensing this, the packed house at Yankee Stadium applauded him for fully five minutes when he went out to center field in the ninth inning.

Later, in the madhouse that was the victorious Yankee dressing room, Stengel pushed through the crowd and grabbed DiMaggio by the arms. Tears ran down the Yankee manager's cheeks. "If it wasn't for you," he said to Joe, "we wouldn't have done it. Joe, this is your title. Yours alone. You did it."

On December 11, the Yankee management called in the press and announced Joe DiMaggio's retirement from baseball. Manager Casey Stengel and a number of Yankee players were on hand for the historic occasion. Before Joe spoke, Yankee owner Dan Topping seemed close to tears. He said, "We tried everything we possibly could to get him to stay. But we couldn't convince him. I don't know why he had to quit. Sick as he was last season he did better than most of the players hanging around."

But playing better than most of the players hanging around never was enough for Joe DiMaggio. "I once made a solemn promise to myself," he said to the writers, "that I wouldn't try to hang on once the end was in sight. I've seen too many beat-up players struggle to stay up there, and it was always a sad spectacle.

"You all know," he continued solemnly, "that I've had more than my share of injuries and setbacks during my career. Lately they've been too frequent and too serious to laugh off. And when baseball is no longer fun, it is no longer a game. So I've played my last game of ball."

Not a few of the veteran sportswriters had trouble seeing their notes through the mist of their eyes as Joe shook hands all around and left the room.

"Well," a writer sighed, "that's that." Then he turned to Stengel. "Say, Case, who's gonna be your outfield next year?"

The Yankee manager scratched his head a moment. "Well, I'll tell you," he said. "We got those two guys we used in right last year, and there's two young fellers we . . ."

But DiMaggio was no longer there to hear them.

22

Retirement came easily to Joe DiMaggio in the spring of 1952. It was the first spring in some seventeen years except for the war years, that he did not have to report to a Yankee training camp, and he was enjoying his newly found leisure. He lived with his widowed sister Marie in a tan stone house on a quiet residential street not far from Fisherman's Wharf. He bought the house for his parents and after their death he made it his home.

He spent most of his mornings in the DiMaggio restaurant on Fisherman's Wharf, where he signed autographs for customers, slowly sipped a cup of coffee, and read the sports pages. He dined with friends, played gin rummy at his club, watched television, went to a local movie, and made plans to return East when the baseball season began, to do Yankee pregame and postgame shows. Back in New York he seemed, for the first time, to enjoy the fact that he was perhaps the biggest celebrity in town.

That spring Gus Zernial of the Philadelphia Athletics was being touted as the "new DiMaggio." He had led the

American League in home runs the previous season, blast-
ing out thirty-three, and was nicknamed Ozark Ike because of his powerful frame. David March, a Hollywood
agent, phoned the Athletics' office one afternoon and arranged a series of publicity pictures with Ozark Ike and
March's new client, a beautiful young actress named
Marilyn Monroe.

The photographic session didn't take more than half an
hour. Marilyn took the bat in her hand and crouched at
home plate. Zernial was told to wrap his arms around her
and show her how to grip the baseball bat.

The pictures of Marilyn Monroe and Gus Zernial were
in all the papers by the next day, and Joe DiMaggio, playing in an exhibition game against the Athletics, kidded
Gus about the pictures with the beautiful Miss Monroe.

"How come I never get to pose with beautiful girls like
that?" Joe said. "I told him that this guy David March was
her agent and arranged it. I guess he called March," said
Zernial.

And so it was David March who arranged for the first
date for Joe and Marilyn, and the beginning of the romance that was tailor-made for every press agent in
America.

March persuaded Marilyn to go to dinner with DiMaggio along with March and his girlfriend, at the Villa Nova
Restaurant in Hollywood.

The date was set for seven o'clock. Marilyn did not appear until nearly nine o'clock.

Joe got up from his chair when she arrived, held out his
hand to greet Marilyn, and then sat down.

There was little, if any, talk between Marilyn and Joe

as the evening progressed. Joe wasn't much of a small talker, and Marilyn kept talking to March about a picture she was making, titled *Monkey Business*.

Joe finally showed animation when Mickey Rooney spotted DiMaggio and joined the party. A baseball fan with real insight into the game, Mickey spoke only to Joe and began to re-create all sorts of famous baseball feats Joe had performed. Marilyn, who pretended to March that she had never heard of DiMaggio, was impressed by the admiration shown by Rooney, a full-blown Hollywood star in his own right.

Just before eleven o'clock that evening, Marilyn announced that she had an early call the next morning and asked to be excused. She smiled her lovely smile at Joe and said, "It's been nice, Joe."

Joe was up from the table at once.

"I'd like to see you home," he said. "I'll get a cab."

"Thank you," Marilyn replied, "but I have my own car. But if you'd like I'll drive you to your hotel."

"That would be very nice of you," said Joe, and Marilyn and Joe walked out of the Villa Nova Restaurant, for the first time together and alone.

In Marilyn's car, for a while, there was little or no conversation. Joe knew little about the motion-picture business, while Marilyn knew less about baseball. They drove in complete silence until they reached the hotel where Joe was staying.

"It's early," said Joe. "I don't feel like turning in yet. Would you mind driving around for a little while?"

"It's a lovely night for a drive," said Marilyn as she headed away from the downtown area.

"My heart jumped," she would say later. "All of a sud-

den I was full of happiness to be with Joe." Marilyn dro
quietly for a few minutes, then turned around, headed
back to Joe's hotel. She repeated that she had to get up
early the next morning. DiMaggio said he would call her
again. She did not answer and drove back to her hotel.

She was already in bed when the phone rang. She answered sleepily.

"This is Joe. Would you care to have dinner with me tomorrow?"

"No," she said flatly. "Thank you very much, but I'm
busy."

"How about the next night?"

"No, I'm busy then too. Call me again sometime."

Joe called again, this time in the afternoon. He called
again that evening. He called her every day, twice and
three times a day for weeks, and she refused every time.
Finally he stopped calling. A week went by. The phone
rang in Joe's hotel suite. It was Marilyn.

"Would you like to take me to dinner tonight?" she
asked.

They began dating regularly. She trusted DiMaggio,
admired his honesty, the shyness that was akin to hers.
His lack of guile and his strength appealed to her. He
gave her strength, and she understood his quiet, dignified
silence.

It was only a matter of a few days before the romance
became public. Their names were in all the gossip columns. Joe dined with her in the best-known restaurants in
San Francisco and in Hollywood. They talked with each
other several times a day on the phone. Soon the rumor
mills had an impending marriage.

And finally, on January 14, 1954, Harry Brand, the publicity director of Twentieth Century-Fox, received a call from Marilyn.

"Harry, Joe and I are getting married this afternoon," she said.

The wedding between Hollywood's glamorous Marilyn Monroe and baseball's most popular hero, Joe DiMaggio, was scheduled to take place in the private chambers of Judge Charles Perry, of the San Francisco Municipal Court, at one thirty in the afternoon. Reno Barsocchini, a longtime DiMaggio friend and at the time manager of the DiMaggio restaurant, made all the hurried arrangements. Reno and Lefty O'Doul and Lefty's wife, along with Marilyn, Joe, and Tom DiMaggio were to be the only people in the judge's chambers. Marilyn wore a brown suit with a white ermine collar and looked beautiful. DiMaggio wore a blue suit and a blue polka-dot tie. The ceremony took but five minutes as hundreds of newsmen, photographers, and curious fans jammed every inch of the courthouse.

Joe and Marilyn pushed through the throng, made their way down the stairs, got into their car with the help of several policemen, and drove off. Three hours later Joe pulled the blue Cadillac off the road at the Clifton Motel in the tiny town of Paso Robles.

Motel owner Ernie Sharpe was watching television as the office door of the motel opened. He looked up and Joe DiMaggio was staring at him.

"Well, I'll be. It's Joe DiMaggio."

"Hi. We'd like a room with a television set."

The following evening, the DiMaggios paid their bill, gave Sharpe their autographs, and drove off to a quiet lodge in the mountains some fifty miles from Palm Springs.

It was a blissful two weeks. The newlyweds would return to San Francisco for a short stay, then continue their honeymoon with a trip to Japan.

Marilyn and Joe flew into Tokyo in January and checked into the Imperial Hotel. The Korean War had just ended, but more than one million United States servicemen still remained in Korea, and when a high-ranking U.S. general asked Marilyn to go to Korea to entertain the GIs she eagerly accepted. Joe was against the trip, but could not keep her from going. Joe was sullen and unhappy about the separation on their honeymoon, and when they returned to America, Marilyn went to work on a new movie, *The Seven Year Itch*.

DiMaggio flew to New York to handle some business. Marilyn flew in a few days later for some scenes for the new picture, and now the rumor mills began to build.

Day after day the Hollywood gossip columnists hinted of an impending break in the marriage. They hinted that Marilyn could never give up her career for a home and family. That was all that DiMaggio wanted. He wanted her to move to San Francisco and raise a family. She wanted him to move to Hollywood and help her in her career.

And so, on October 5, 1954, just 274 days after they were married, Marilyn Monroe and Joe DiMaggio agreed to separate. Shortly thereafter, Marilyn was granted a divorce.

And so they parted as friends. And they remained close friends and saw each other frequently until Marilyn's tragic death early in 1962.

23

The usual late-evening crowd was gathered at "the store," as the regulars call Toots Shor's restaurant. Show-business personalities, political bigwigs, sports figures, writers, and newspaper people all collected to gossip and talk shop.

At one table sat the proprietor, Toots himself, with a couple of sportswriters, a movie press agent, and Joe DiMaggio. Since his retirement from the Yankees four years before, Joe had been connected with several different business enterprises and had tried TV sportscasting for a while after his marriage to Marilyn Monroe. Now he was back in probably the only place he ever felt really comfortable, and with the only people with whom he could feel at ease, away from a ball field.

That day Joe had received a singular honor. He had been elected to the Baseball Hall of Fame. When he received his plaque at Cooperstown, New York, he said, "This closes the book." But his friends at the table now were reluctant to close the book on the career of the Yankee Clipper. Their coffee was growing cold as they recalled incidents that stood out in their minds. But soon they saw that Joe was embarrassed by their discussion of him, and they switched the subject.

"What do you do with yourself now, Joe?" Earl Wilson, columnist of the New York *Post*, asked.

Joe kind of shrugged. "I keep pretty busy. I've got Edward Bennett Williams, of Washington, handling some investments for me. I'm doing a couple of TV commercials for a coffee-maker company and a New York bank that keeps me pretty busy, and they're nice people to work with."

One of the sportswriters shook his head. "It's not like playing baseball, eh, Joe?"

DiMaggio smiled. "What is? But then, I don't hurt all over when I get up in the morning, either."

A show-business agent who knew Joe pretty well joined the table. "Congratulations, Joe," he said to DiMaggio. "They should have put you in the Hall of Fame years ago."

"I'm happy enough to be in it at all," Joe replied.

"Yeah, well, listen, Joe. I've got something lined up for you if you want. Ten thousand a week for personal appearances here in New York, Chicago, and San Francisco. Two weeks in each town. You make sixty thousand in six weeks. Bad?"

Joe looked at him. "What would I do?"

"Just tell a couple of stories, funny ones about baseball, you know. And take your bow."

"I'm a former ballplayer, not a circus freak," Joe said.

A couple of autograph seekers came over, and Joe, appearing as embarrassed as ever over the procedure, signed his name. Then a waiter appeared and told him there was a telephone call for him.

When he had gone, Shor shook his head sadly. "Today should be one of the biggest days of his life. He's elected to the Hall of Fame, and he comes in here and sits around with us. And you know something? As soon as he got back from Cooperstown he called me up to see if I was free to have dinner with him tonight. If I wasn't, he'd be eating alone somewhere, in some spaghetti joint."

One of the sportswriters shrugged. "What else does he have to do? His investments are paying off, he can take it easy. He likes it that way."

Shor talked on, as if he hadn't heard the interruption. "He comes in twice, maybe three times a week for lunch. And he sits alone and eats it, unless I sit down for a cup of coffee with him. Comes in at night, too, a lot, which I like, mind you, 'cause I love Joe like a brother. But almost always he's alone. A guy like him, you'd think he'd have to shake 'em off, and at least have a girl with him all the time. But always he's alone."

"He's one of the nicest guys I ever met," the other sportswriter said. "I've known him since he came up in '36. We get along fine. But I still wouldn't call myself a close friend of his. I hardly know anybody besides you who could call himself a good friend of his, Toots."

"He's a strange guy, Joe is," the restaurateur said. "Spends too much time worrying about things, thinking about the past. He's always afraid he'll say or do something that'll make him look silly and get in the papers. It's okay to have pride, but sometimes I think Joe whips himself to death with it."

DiMaggio returned from his phone call, and the conversation switched quickly to another subject. "Business,"

Joe said, explaining the call. Then he looked at his watch. "Well, I think I'll be going home."

"What for?" Shor said. "It's pretty early yet. Whatta you got to do tomorrow?"

"I had a big day today. Traveled to Cooperstown and all that." He picked up the plaque awarded him at the Hall of Fame ceremonies. "Now I need a good night's sleep." He waved good-bye to everyone at the table and walked out into the hot July night. They all looked after him.

"There," said one of the sportswriters, "goes one of the greatest players in the history of baseball."

"And one of the greatest guys," said the other sportswriter.

"And one of the loneliest men in the world," said Toots Shor.

INDEX

GENE SCHOOR has been associated with sports and sports personalities since his high school days in Passaic, New Jersey. After winning a number of amateur boxing championships in New Jersey, Gene received an athletic scholarship to Miami University (Florida) where the boxing team became contenders for the national championships during the years that Schoor was a member of the team. Gene captured some eighteen regional boxing championships and fought his way to the final round of the 1948 Olympics as a welterweight, only to lose his post on the team due to a broken hand.

Mr. Schoor has been a teacher and boxing coach at both the University of Minnesota and City College, New York, and was also a sports commentator on radio stations WINS, WNBC, and WHN. He has produced and directed radio and television programs with Joe DiMaggio and Jack Dempsey. Currently, he is devoting his efforts to his writing career and has published a number of books with the best-selling author, Robin Moore. The author of forty books, Schoor has written biographies of many of the nation's greatest sports and political figures including: *Vince Lombardi—Football's Greatest Coach, Bob Feller—Strikeout King, The Story of Yogi Berra, The Jackie Robinson Story, The Jim Thorpe Story, The Story of Willie Mays, Leo Durocher, Young John Kennedy, Young Robert Kennedy, The Story of Franklin D. Roosevelt, General Douglas MacArthur, Sugar Ray Robinson, Roy Campanella, Treasury of Notre Dame Football, Treasury of Army-Navy Football,* and other books of note.

Schoor, Gene

Joe DiMaggio

197

800314